MW00952572

The Ultimate High:
A Memoir

CHRISTINA GIORDANO

Copyright © 2018 Christina Giordano

All rights reserved.

ISBN: 1717161189
ISBN-13: 978-1717161185

DEDICATION

Firstly, and *always* first, this book belongs to God, my Lord and Savior, Jesus Christ and the Holy Spirit. Forever I will praise your Glory and declare Your goodness and the mercy you have bestowed upon me. I am the witness to your undying love and the miracles you have shown me. You called me out of the grave and gave me life. For that I am forever your faithful servant.

Secondly, I dedicate this book to my *The Magnificent Seven*. These are the seven people that saved my life. If it weren't for each of them and their pivotal roles in my life, I would not be here. Each one of you have contributed to my life and the beauty it now holds. There are no words that can express my thankfulness and gratitude to each of you. You took my life in your hands and made sure I didn't fail. I love you guys so much.

The Magnificent Seven are:

Cheryl, D'Agostino, Cindy Vaughn, Brent Legere, Anne Marie Lago, Kimberly Bigelow, Celeste Mollica and Matt Vyhnanek.

And to all my fellow Valhalla Vikings, you kept me as part of the Viking Family all these years after high school and have become an incredible support system. It was an honor to share my childhood with each and every one of you. I love you all from my heart to yours.

To my beautiful editor Lisa Stalvey Coady. This book wouldn't be what it is if it wasn't for you. I have grown very fond of the word "extrapolate" because you pushed me to dig into the deepest parts of my journey, which was painful, and where I didn't necessarily want to go. It took a lot of stomping your feet a few times to get me to do it, and I'm glad you did. There is no way I could ever thank you enough for the countless hours of work you have done for me. I love you.

To my sister in spirit across the Atlantic Ocean in Australia, Amy Huq. Your unfailing and faithful friendship all these years is one that I will always treasure. Thank you for the endless phone calls, your support and help with the title of this memoire.

CHRISTINA GIORDANO

TABLE OF CONTENTS

THE ULTIMATE HIGH: A MEMOIR

INTRODUCTION

During the last eighteen months, I've had time to reflect on my life. The good, the bad, the ugly, the beautiful and the unknown. While this memoir is primarily about the turbulent lifestyle I've lived, up until my awakening with God, I can't help but reflect on everything that's happened and how far I have come. Grace and mercy is a gift. It is given to us freely. God does not keep a tally of your sins, nor does he condemn you for them. My passion lies with God himself and his son Jesus Christ. Without my belief and faith in them I am nothing. My life and what could have been the loss of my life would mean absolutely nothing and that is a scary truth. My hope is that, while I can't save the world, maybe someone will read this book and be spared his or her pain of addiction. On the flip side of that, for the person who is distraught about a loved one being plagued by this mad lifestyle to be able to understand how the addict feels. The thing is, we don't want to feel when we are in active addiction. It's easier to numb the pain and hide ourselves behind a make-believe life that has no meaning. Essentially, we're just waiting to die and hoping that next fix is the one that does us in. If what happened to me saves just one life, then that is what this was all for.

***

The turbulent wake of chaos that we leave behind is most often worse than the addiction itself. But while traveling down that long dark tunnel, if by chance you can see even a little tiny sparkle of light, run. Run to it as fast as you can because what's waiting on the other side is one of the most beautiful miracles you will ever experience. Trust me, I'm an addict. This memoir started out as my personal journal documenting my recovery for myself. Then I realized, with the help of my best friend Cheryl nagging me for a decade, someone needs to read this. Is it just a documented amount of copious drug use and partying? No, it isn't. It's a story about a little girl that once held the whole world in her hands and just like grains of sand, she watched it all fall through her fingers. But hope remains. And I hope that whoever reads this finds strength from it. You all were fearlessly and wonderfully made, and while the disease of drug addiction has no prejudice, it does possess free will. God gave us that choice. Today I choose my sobriety and recovery over anything else. It is that important to me and my hope is someday it will be that important to you.

~Christina Giordano

FOREWARD

Most of us have that *one* friend. You know, the one who always draws attention to themselves. The one who needs to write a book because nobody can believe that all this *shit* happens to one person! Well, Christina is this one friend. She is unapologetically of who she is – take it or leave it. Unfortunately, as you will see, most folks try to both take *and* leave it. But, I'm getting ahead of myself.

Christina and I met in the early 1970's in Kindergarten. I can't recall whether we were friends first and introduced our parents, or vice versa. Either way, we spent lots of time together throughout our early years. Her parents, Joe and Diane, were the kind of couple that you notice. Diane was absolutely stunning and Joe a perfect compliment. I have many memories of the large Giordano family. Kids running around the backyard getting a bee sting in my foot, playing 'teacher' to Christina's sister in their ginormous downstairs play area, or trying to sneak into the wine cellar.

Chris and I have been friends ever since, and though geographically challenged for many years, we have an unusual bond. We are, not surprisingly, complete opposites – and not just in looks either! She is a skinny brunette and well, I'm not! Where I tend to stay in the shadows, Chris seeks and craves the attention of the spotlight. Except for singing in the shower, there is nothing musical about me. Music is Christina's forte. Her voice is beautiful and she can bring life to almost any instrument. Before the beginning of the end, she was living the *'rock and roll'* lifestyle. Me, on the other hand, married into a nice, sort of quiet Italian family while Chris owns the NY Italian stereotype. Lastly, while I feel incredibly blessed to have found and married the love of my life, Christina's life has been a chameleonic journey of misdirection, continually following the path where love was most plausible. SO, buckle up and enjoy the ride! It's a bumpy one! As you read her story, bear in mind that she is opening her heart, mind, and soul to the reader. Many times, swallowing her big *'eye-talian'* pride to show the truth. As her friend, I ask a favor. Do not be quick to judge. Mistakes have been made, prices paid.

~Cheryl D'Agostino

THE ULTIMATE HIGH: A MEMOIR

CHAPTER 1

NOT ENOUGH

***

Not that we are sufficient in ourselves to claim anything coming from us, but our sufficiency is from God. ~2 Corinthians 3:5

I wasn't always an addict, in fact I had a pretty decent home life in the suburb of White Plains in Westchester County, New York. My Family were immigrants from Italy and they managed to carve out a pretty decent legacy to carry on. I emerged into this world on January 3, 1970. I was a colic baby actually losing my voice while crying. My parents said I was the epitome of 'pain- in- the- ass' baby; up all night crying and fussing. I suppose at that point I considered myself a burden, not good enough, but who the hell knows what made even think about using drugs. My parents were the epitome of the happily married couple living the American dream. My mother was a pure-bred Italian beauty with the most gorgeous hazel eyes. When she entered a room, it was with grace and poise. You actually had no choice but to look at her. My father was always working.

1

He missed most of my childhood due to the busy life style of being one of the most sought-after musicians on the New York City circuit. My father taught me to play baseball in the back yard when he was home on those rare occasions and my mom was a fantastic cook. We lived in the biggest house in the neighborhood, a beautiful three-story stone front house with almost an acre of land. We were pretty high up in Italian society as my family had ties to organized crime families and we were what you would call, always cared for. We were well versed as to the proper way to do things like which fork to eat from first and how to hold your pinky perfectly as you sipped your tea. And most important, always remember to spoon your soup from inside of the cup to the outside of the cup, and for God sake, do not slurp! So, what did I do during those one hundred dollar a plate dinners at Tavern On The Green? I picked up my bowl of soup and I slurped it all down in one gulp.

I was the rebel in my family and the one that always got into trouble. Some call that the *'black sheep'* of the family. I was always grounded or had things taken away from me to 'teach me a lesson'. All of my friends at school were popular and liked while I was the little fat friend that tagged along. I got teased and bullied, but I kept trudging on. I found solace in music at a very young age. I was in fourth grade when I was introduced to the flute. Oh, the beautiful fairy like classical sound it made took my breath away. I found my calling. I was going to follow in my father's footsteps and carry on the legacy of being a musician. I was always in the 1st flute section, but for some reason I always played second chair to a little nerd boy. Who would've thought a boy played the flute? Not me! Boys played 'manly' instruments like the saxophone or the trumpet! *Not the flute*! I wasn't good enough for 1st chair, 1st Flute. I was always in the 2nd chair.

***

After graduation, I accepted a partial scholarship to *The Julliard School of Music*, a very prestigious honor. By this time, I had mastered multiple instruments ranging from violin, piano, viola, clarinet, piccolo, oboe and my voice. It was inevitable that music was calling me. However, as life went on, I chased after a dream that was very acrimonious and fragile. My family moved to Marco Island, Florida around this time, so I would come down for summer during school breaks. Then one summer I met Rob, an insanely handsome man. He had dark hair, dark eyes and fair complexion. He was a Marine who served and protected our country in the Middle East. He was disciplined and fun all at the same time. He made my heart sing. I was falling in love, secretly hoping he'd ask me to marry him one day. We continued dating for eighteen months, when it happened; he finally asked me to marry him, and of course I said yes! He was the man I always wanted to be with. It was a plus he supported my music and me. My father loved him like a son and my mother adored him. But then my perfect world came tumbling down on me and suddenly that would subsequently affect me in the most unexpected and profound way. A month before we were going be married, Rob committed suicide, shooting himself in the head. There are no words to explain the loss, despair and deep pain I was in, and obviously stayed in for years afterwards. He was to be my husband for the rest of my life. I was going to have children with him. The devastation I felt then and still do now, is inexplicable. I'm not sure I've truly healed from that event and although the pain subsides, the memory is always there. Unbeknownst to anyone or me it was later revealed he suffered from PTSD from the war, *Operation Desert Storm*. I wasn't enough to keep him from pulling the trigger. Again, it was my fault, I wasn't good enough for him to live, or so I thought. I found solace and numbness after that with drugs. It was great to never have to feel those painful emotions again. The amazing feeling of numbness and simultaneous idea that you are the most important person in the world, became the double extravaganza that would become my life for the next couple of years. In 1991 everything got a tad out of control, actually *way* out of control. On the night of my twenty-first birthday, a few friends rented a limousine and naturally we made sure we had four eight balls of cocaine ready to snort. We were ready to seriously party! We had a great time, at least I think we did. Everything seems way more fun screwed up for some reason, like you've accomplished something super important. Unfortunately, it's all in your head! I was going to turn twenty-one years old and this is how I chose to do it, and to this day I don't remember a thing.

I do know this though; I woke up the following morning in my bed, in my apartment on Marco Island in my own urine and feces. It was disgusting. I still have no idea how I got there. And more interestingly, I had no idea who the guy in my bed was either. I'd never seen him before in my life. Oh my God, did we have sex? Did I get an STD? I was out of control. I called my mother, Diane and begged her not to put me in rehabilitation for drugs, but now in retrospect, I should have begged to go to one. She came to my apartment, picked me up and didn't know anything about the detox I was about to go through. She did know I was using drugs though. I'd overheard a conversation on the phone between my mom and my roommate, Katie the day before. Katie, at the time, was a prissy little prude with mousey brown hair and a smirk of a smile that just wreaked of egotism. She was always trying to get one up on everyone else and really, we just used her to run drugs for us. She didn't party at all and if she did it wasn't like us. To my circle, and me she was quite boring but tried to fit in by running the drugs where we needed her to because she was such a goody-two shoes looking girl that no one would ever suspect her carrying drugs. Katie called my mom the morning of my twenty-first birthday. When I overheard her talking and realized it was my mom she was speaking to, I picked up my phone quietly and heard Katie rat me out.

"Mrs. Giordano, it's Katie, Christina's roommate," she said in that annoyingly mousy voice of hers. "I just thought you should know that your daughter is using drugs and it's getting out of control. There's people here partying all the time and I can't handle it. She's messed up all the time."

My mother's response was eloquent and powerful and until this day I can still hear her voice on the other end of the phone.

"I know that Katie. You aren't telling me anything I do not know. But my daughter turns twenty-one today. She isn't a child anymore. It is her choice if she wants to do drugs. I can only help her if she helps herself. Until then, it doesn't matter if she hurts you, her father or me. The only thing I can do at this point is wait until she falls and pray that she is able to come back."

I hung up the phone quietly after that comment from my mom. What they spoke about afterwards is a mystery to me. Although considering I never saw Katie again, I would assume it was about her moving out. One thing was for sure, I wasn't going to let her or my mom ruin my twenty-first birthday. However, the dude upstairs with the white robe and flip-flops on, sitting on His gold throne in the clouds has a real strange sense of humor. I'm talking about God, in case you were wondering, and God bless mom for not putting me in rehab. I managed to remain clean from drugs for nearly twenty-five years after that day. I went back to school at Juilliard for one more semester and my dreams of being a world-renowned classical musician were shattered once again, very suddenly and painfully.

***

My mother, at the young age of forty-five years old came down with cancer, and within seven months, she was gone. When my mom was diagnosed, she and my dad kept it a secret from my sister and me for three months. They said the reason for this was that they didn't want to ruin my twenty-second birthday and I had a considerably rough time getting and staying clean that previous year, not to mention the added chaos of losing Rob. They just really wanted me to enjoy my birthday. Then, on January 6th, 1992, mom sat me down on the couch in our family room and told me what type of cancer she had and sadly it was lung cancer. Back then, there wasn't the medical advances they have now to operate on my mom, but if it had been operable, she would be alive today. She noted that chemotherapy would be starting the following week and assured me she was going to beat this disease and get better. When she was well enough again she promised we would be making that trip back to New York for a mother-daughter shopping spree in the city, something we had always planned to do but never had the time do it. I watched her deteriorate rapidly every day for the next four months. I would have the night shift as my father had to work during the day. I would be up all night with mom talking and helping her to stand up to go to the bathroom. We would talk about the past and about the future. We talked about that damn shopping spree in New York City that never happened. I now cherish those moments with her. So many conversations we had and so many amends that took place. I remember apologizing to her,

"Mom, I'm so sorry for being such a rotten kid. I'm sorry for all the pain I caused you while I was growing up." I said as a tear rolled down my face.

She chuckled, "My sweet Chrissy, you weren't rotten. You were just lost and it's ok. You've made me proud to be your mom."

She died in my arms two days later. It was the most horrifying and painful death I'd ever seen. Her lungs had literally collapsed and as she gasped for air in my arms. I watched her suffocate to death. She was bone thin and in tremendous pain. Thank God for morphine. This experience sent me spiraling down emotionally, but I internalized it. During one of our late-night conversations a few days before she asked me to take care of my sister, she asked me to make sure she finished college. She asked me to be strong for my father and accept the fact that he was young and would possibly want to be with someone else someday. I had been awarded the dying wish of my mother and the luxury of taking care of everyone else and their feelings. No one ever thinks his or her mom or dad will die. The mortality in me emerged and slapped me in the face and not in a good way. I was only twenty-two years old and this wasn't supposed to happen. She was supposed to get better. The night she died, I drove to the Catholic Church down the street, running in frantically down the center aisle, yelling and screaming at the image of Christ nailed to a cross hanging above the alter. I threw every bible I could get my hands on at Him, trying to knock Him down. *I was pissed!* This wasn't fair! He, the supposed Divine Being, took my mother, my music, Rob and everything I loved away from me. I told Him that He was nothing, a fake magician with a fantastic stupid little book that told a silly fairy tale. I told Him if He were here, I would've hammered the nails into His hands myself. To my surprise, as hard as I threw those fairy tale books at him and being a pretty good shortstop, He remained hanging above the alter. I stormed out of that church ready to take on the world and become the force that everyone would bow to. From that moment on, I was never going to let anyone ever hurt me and get away with it. I vowed to crush any human, plant or animal that would do me harm. My dark side emerged from the bowels of hell. I became the image of evil. Hells fire ran though my veins as I pushed those wooden doors of that church out in front of me. As I emerged from the church with my vengeance against God I stood on the steps with my fists raised to the sky with a blood curdling scream coming from the bowls of hell in my soul. I also had a strong feeling God wasn't done with me yet. In fact, He had only just begun.

***

A week after my mom died, dad sat me down for a talk. It was to be my most unselfish decision that I had ever made. He began with how proud he was of me, my musical accomplishments and how my tenure at Julliard was what he always wanted for me. Alas, now that my mother was gone, he could only afford either my sister or me to go back to school, not both. I graciously accepted my defeat. I understood this because my father had only one income coming in now. He explained to me that my mother's life insurance policy was small and not enough to cover the expenses. My father assured me that he would personally help me to continue my education as a musician. After all, he had a Master's Degree in music and was an extremely accomplished musician. That promise didn't last long as the alcohol and grief of losing my mother consumed him. My father was drinking himself to death so he could see my mother as soon as possible. He would salute his cocktail to her picture every night and say, "See you soon D." I asked him one night if he would like to date a woman again someday. He always had the best euphemisms. I would actually call them Joe-isms. His response was very dramatic, but in a bad rendition of a drunken Hamlet sort of way.

"My darling child. I have drunk the *finest* of champagnes for the past 26 years. Why on God's green Earth would I *ever* go to drinking draft beer?"

That was the best analogy of love coming from an alcoholic that I had ever heard. It seemed to me that when you love ultimately and unconditionally, they are the love of your life, they are yours in body, mind and soul. You have this intense connection that nothing in this world can break and no one will understand unless they've been there. I think that's what's been the void in me most of my life. Finding love that intense and someone who is genuinely in love with me as much as I am with them, I think this may have been Rob but unfortunately, I'll never know that. I laugh and think to myself, *"I can love like that"*. But I always look at myself, as I'm not enough. Time went on as it normally does. At the time of my mother's death, I was dating a great guy named Brandon. Damn he was sexy! Again, just like Rob, he had dark hair, dark eyes and a pale complexion. He was a great chef at one of the local restaurants and my parents liked him. My mother always said he had the best smile she had ever seen. Brandon stayed by my side with my mom the night she died. He'd been through the pain of losing his father so he knew how it felt to lose a parent. He didn't come with me for my cursing session with Christ at the Catholic Church that night, but while I was sitting on the outside step of the church to clear my head after my screaming subsided, in my fucked-up mind I suddenly thought, *"Jesus, Life is too short. I've got to get everything done that I want to do very quickly before I die!"* So, I went to work on that whole idea of getting shit done rapidly. I went straight back to Brandon with a soap box stance and tears in my eyes.

"Life is too short to be wasting my time Brandon. You need to make a choice. You either marry my ass by next year or I'm done with this relationship. I have to get shit done and I won't let you hold me back!".

He looked at me in total amazement, paused for a second and then took a deep breath, "Well, I'm not about to lose you now so let's get married. But your dad is Italian so I need to ask him first."

And so, we were married on May 18th, 1994 and divorced two years later. To this day, Brandon and I are still friends. He is a constant support of my sobriety and a confidant of great measure. In a very recent conversation with him he said to me, "Chris, don't you wish someone would've smacked are heads together before we got married and said *what the fuck are you two thinking?*" Only Brandon and my dad were ever allowed to call me Chris.

"Yeah, maybe. But if they did, then I probably would've never been the awesome first ex-wife I am today. I would've been just another girlfriend."

Four years later after Brandon and I were divorced, I bought a horse farm in Naples, Florida. My mother loved horses. My dad always said that if she were alive he would never see her because she would always be at my ranch riding, bathing and grooming my horses. It was a serene environment for me. It was just me and my horses in the middle of nowhere. But still, it wasn't enough. On my quest to find that unconditional love, Larry entered my life. He wasn't the greatest looking guy. In fact, he wasn't handsome at all. He had an annoying southern twang, the typical North Carolina southern drawl. He had blonde hair and blue eyes and oh, did I mention he was homely looking as well? He was kind to me though and took care of me. He truly seemed to love me unconditionally. I quickly adapted that old saying, '*Looks aren't everything.*' So, when he asked me to marry him, I said yes. I loved him back then as best as I could until he revealed to me he was much worse of an alcoholic than my father was. He was the most violent alcoholic I had ever come in contact with.

I managed to keep my family out of this hell for 4 years, but I couldn't take it any longer. I'd had enough of him and ended up sending him to prison for 5 years. It was a very painful experience and one that I never wanted to get too detailed about. I suppressed a lot of that emotion and pain over the years. It was the way I was able to protect myself and my family. Why I stayed with him as long as I did is beyond me. I needed the right moment to get away from him. That one moment when you just know. The freedom I felt knowing he was out of my life was a relief, this is why I got my concealed weapons permit just in case he decided to come back after his five years behind bars. That's a lot of time to think about things and I couldn't be sure he'd not want to hurt me when he got out. My family as I had mentioned, was involved in organized crime years back but we still had a few ties. Through the grapevine of Naples, Florida, I heard that Larry had a problem with his kneecaps while he was in prison, if you get my drift. I decided I'd stay on at the ranch for a few more years. It was my peaceful place. That idea didn't last long as it was only a few months later that I would begin another nose dive of my dreams. On November 15th, 2009, I got a call from my dad during the late-night hours. It wasn't a good one either.

"Chrissy, I've fallen and my head is split open. I'm bleeding all over the place", he said calmly but with slurred speech on the phone. I knew he'd been drinking.

"Dad, are you alright? How much blood is there?" I said knowing that sometimes my father had a way of exaggerating things especially when he was drunk.

"I don't know, but it doesn't look good"

"Ok. I'm on my way

My dad lived forty-five minutes away from me, I couldn't understand why he didn't call my sister. She lived right down the street from him, for Christ sakes! Oh, but I forgot, she was the perfect child, always doing the right things all the time. She had the husband with the pension plan and retirement set in place. And, then there were their two beautiful little girls, the Golden Retriever and the 'white–picket- fence- lifestyle.' She was also more interested in her social status than she was her family; and my father and I didn't fit in to that category. As much as she didn't like to admit it, she was *exactly* like my mother's mother; most of you would call that a Grandmother. That woman was anything but.

**

As I was thinking about all these things rushing through my head while driving to my dad, one question kept coming back to me. Why me? Why am I always the one called upon to help others? And when I need something, no one seems to even acknowledge I'm alive. Again, I must not be enough. How boring, right? I rushed like a maniac down S.R. 951 not knowing what I was going to walk into. When I walked up the stairs to my father's house it was like I was in the *Texas Chainsaw Massacre,* where they'd just finished filming a horrific scene. Blood was splattered on the walls. Hand smears of blood were on the doors and doorknobs. There was a huge pool of blood on the floor and broken glass everywhere. He'd fallen through the glass coffee table in the living room; head first. At this point most people would freak out. I sat him on the couch, called 911 and began taking his pulse. For some reason, my Dad thought I was this amazing person that could just sew his head up and be done with it. That wasn't going to happen that night. We arrived at the hospital and miraculously my sister came with me. She actually took the time out of her busy schedule to tend to her father. When the doctor came out to see us we were told dad's alcohol level was at 1.8. So, in reality he had alcohol poisoning. That left him with forty-two internal stitches and twenty-seven staples in his head that came graciously down his forehead. He was in surprisingly good spirits.

"Hey old man, how are you feeling?" I said with a chuckle in my voice.

"Pretty good I think. But I'm sure I'm going to have a headache in the morning"

"Ya, think? Christ, you look like Frankenstein. Let's get out of here"

We brought Dad home. He swore off all alcohol. He dumped every last drop left in the house down the drain and refused to ever drink again. That lasted 90 days. Again, I would be giving up my dreams. This time, and for the next 5 years, I would be taking care of my hero- my dad. My dad's alcoholism continued and I kept thinking about that old saying in my head, '*You can't teach and old dog new tricks.*' I moved in with my dad to take care of him for a while and lost my horse farm to foreclosure. It was 2009 and the market took a hard dive, I couldn't even short sale it. The years went on and on and I was sort of able to get some recognition in the small community of Marco Island City and was asked to sing *The National Anthem* for the Florida Everglades Hockey team, the Fort Myers Miracle baseball team, The Minnesota Twins Spring Training, the New York Yankees spring training as well as the Tampa Bay Rays and Tampa Bay Lightning. My claim to *The National Anthem* fame was singing for the New York Rangers at Madison Square Garden. So, I was sort of a big fish in a small pond. But it wasn't enough. It was never enough. Where the hell did this all come from? I always knew I was meant for more. I've spent my whole life taking care of everyone and not enough time taking care of me. Also, I didn't think most appreciated me for what I was trying to do and didn't think I was worthy of helping others. I supported their dreams and their issues and was there for them. I never did it for myself, ever. I gave up all my dreams and aspirations to make people love me. After a while I felt useless, or should I say used. It was becoming such a routine in my life that I suppose I really didn't logically know any other way to live. The only one I never regretted taking care of was my dad. He was my hero. He pissed me the fuck off a lot, but he was still my hero. One morning while he was having his morning coffee out on the back porch, I came to him and apologized to him for being such a rebellious and out of control kid. He would always answer me using quotes of music or literature when he didn't know what to say. That day he responded to me with the most profound statement that till this day I say to myself in the mirror every morning.

"Every saint has a past, every sinner has a future"

The quote was by Oscar Wilde, and now it adorns the inside of my right forearm as a tattoo. I look at it often and it reminds me of that day my father said it to me. It also reminds me that he died just two days after he said it, which is a very bittersweet memory.

CHAPTER 2

IT'S ONLY ME

***

None of us lives to himself alone. If we live, we live to the Lord; and if we die, we die to the Lord. So, whether we live or die, we belong to the Lord. ~ Romans 14:7-8

We all have a constant in our lives, whether it's a person, place or thing. It's something that without a doubt we can always count on. Something or someone that is always there when times get tough when you feel like your world is falling apart. For me, it was always my dad and my music. I wanted to be just like my dad in the music world and I almost actually achieved it.

Dad was a world-renowned studio musician, acquiring his Masters in Music from New York University in Manhattan. His main forte was percussion, but that man could play everything from the violin to bassoon. He was a band and orchestra director for Emerson High School in Yonkers, New York by day and played in some of the most prestigious clubs in New York City at night. When major celebrities were in town and needed musicians to cover their bands, my father was the one they called. He had a whimsical way about him that all the big names liked and the reason they enjoyed working with him. He played with amazing talents such as Frank Sinatra, Tony Bennett, Dean Martin, Mel Tomei, and a slew of others. Celebrities always surrounded me and until this day, I rarely lose my shit over any celebrity. My thinking is this; they eat, sleep and shit just like I do. They just happen to make a lot more money and are better known than me. One of my dads' favorite stories he always loved to tell me was when he worked on Broadway; there was a little girl about six years old who was in the chorus of the original production of Annie in 1976.

He told it like this, "She was the smallest orphan out of the lot. When she'd come out on stage for the first time every night, she'd look straight at me in the pits with the biggest smile on her tiny little face. I'd wink at her, smiling back and say to myself, *'That's daddy's little girl'*.

His stories always made me feel special and loved. The *'pits'* my dad was referring to comes from the full name, *'Orchestra Pit'*. It's located on the lowered front part of the stage where the music is conducted and played. And you guessed it correctly, that little girl he was referring to was little 'ole me. I was smiling at my hero."

***

Obviously, at one point in my life I *was* actually enough. I was loved and I was greatness personified in my father's eyes. I could do no wrong. And consequently, in my eyes, he could do no wrong. We pissed each other off a lot, though. Being musicians, plus father and daughter, there was a lot of heated debates between us. Creative people are like this quite often. When I was little and couldn't sleep, I would sneak down to my father's music room and prop myself up against the closed door and listen to him practice his instruments, or just be close to him while he was writing music late at night. I know, I couldn't *hear* him writing, but it was my solace. He was my life.

My father taught me to never take shit from anyone. He often said I was the only girl he ever met that had a set of brass balls on her. I didn't grasp what this truly meant at all in my youth and as it turned out, as strong as people thought I was in my later years, I was just the opposite. I was scared to death, acting out in rage and pretending I had it all together. All that show of a strong attitude was a mask. Dad also taught me that the entire world is a stage and we are merely the chorus. The meaning behind this didn't come to me until recently.

I was high up in the local music society until I started using drugs, then everyone scattered. Unless you have something that everyone else wants or everyone else envies, you are literally nothing to them. In this lifetime, you come in contact with people that make impressions, and you come in contact with people that make scars. It's up to you to decide which one they will leave you with. My father left me with both. I wish I could paint a 'holier than thou' picture of my father, but since no one is a saint in this world, I can't. Even though he was my world, he wasn't always nice. I remember one incident, back in high school after my mother was diagnosed with immune thrombocytopenic purpura, or low blood platelets. When I was fifteen years old, we moved to this little town in Pennsylvania called, *New Freedom*. I thought it was hysterical that it was named like the women's feminine hygiene products, but that was my warped way of thinking. It was such a culture shock for me that at fifteen years young, and smack dab in the middle of high school, I was uprooted away from my childhood friends. Everything I knew so dear and familiar to me changed instantly. Now I was living in a small town where the highlight of people's existence was going to church on Sunday morning. Not to say that's bad, but it's the complete opposite of where I came from. I went from pigeons and pollution to chicken coops and corn fields. Looking back, it was actually healthier to get away from the city and it's pollutants. But my God, I've never seen so many fucking corn fields in one place in all my life! I was dating a high school bad boy called Bill, and unfortunately, he introduced me to sex, drugs and rock and roll. Back in the 80's, we called these kinds of people 'Burn Outs' or 'Heads.' In a flash, there I was catapulted from New York's high society, to a small school in a backasswards town. Intrigued by my new fellow classmates, I saw them as backwards. They didn't know any better than the corn fields that surrounded them, which in retrospect it was a snobby thing to say or think. As I sat there in my science class next to the window on the first day attending Susquehannock High School, I stared out the window to the large pasture and cornfields. As I did this, a cow actually walked by and stuck his head in the window while munching on grass. What in God's name? There was actually a cow in the window! I screamed, "Holy Shit!" and promptly on that first day of school got sent to the principal's office for cursing. Not one of my friends in New York would ever believe this. Good Lord, the school was smack-dab in the middle of a cow pasture and a corn field.

***

When my mother was first diagnosed, they said it was Leukemia. We thought we were going to lose her then. Distraught and wanting to escape the reality of the situation, I turned all my energy towards 'Bad Boy Bill', but the day before my mother got out of the hospital, Bill broke up with me. Once again, I was rejected. Life was spinning like a top for me. I was in a strange land with strange people. Even though I had some new friends, they weren't like my New York friends. To add to this situation, my mom was sick and my dad was distant. Further, I had girls five times the size of me bullying me, stalking me at my high school wanting to beat the shit out of me. I was 100% out of my comfort zone. I needed something to take away my pain. This, as I recall, was the first time I didn't want to be alive. I felt that if I was gone, it would be a burden lifted from everyone and everything. I wore all black to school the following morning. Somebody asked me why and my prompt response I think was, "Cause I'm going to a funeral". With no feeling at all, I suddenly realized I was losing my mind, but didn't care. I stuck a razor blade in my pocket as I was walking out of the house that morning, and decided it was time. I ran into the girl's bathroom and began to slice my wrists open. To this day, I don't know what the hell made me lose my mind at that moment. Was it attention I wanted? Did I really want to die? Did I want my parents to see the pain I was in? I told them how unhappy I was about leaving, but it didn't matter to them. I must have been screaming because the school nurse ran into the girl's bathroom and jumped the stall door to rescue me, I was out of my mind crying and screaming. There was blood *everywhere*. I was totally numb. I had no feelings or emotions at all. I remember looking at my friend Misty when the nurse was rushing me out of the bathroom. She had her hand over her mouth in astonishment and was crying. I looked at the crowd that had gathered around the girls bathroom door and everyone's mouth was dropped open. I looked down at my wrists and I finally felt no pain. It was so peaceful. Like I released all my suffering. Now you all can finally *see* my pain. The nurse wrapped my wrists in bandages and called my mother. Misty stayed with me in the nurses office. She was literally the closest person I had there in that backwards town. Misty was a beautiful athletic girl with gorgeous blond hair and eyes as blue as the sky. She had been there for me when I felt alone and she reminded me so much of my best friend Cheryl that I had left in New York. Misty and I were inseparable in high school. We always hung out together and we were always there for each other. Til this day we are still close friends. Very recently we were reunited after 30 years of not seeing each other and just like peas and carrots, nothing had changed between us. We picked up right where we left off. We were the best of friends and still are today. I call her my PA Bestie. The PA stands for Pennsylvania.

***

Thank God the cuts weren't too deep in my wrists, avoiding the emergency room. While waiting for mom to come, I knew she was going to want to kick my ass for this. But she didn't. She and my dad calmly decided to put me away for thirty days in a teenage psychiatric unit in York Hospital. You want to talk about some messed up people. Some of these kids were just down at the bottom rung, way beyond my wildest imagination could I've envisioned such destitution and sickness. I certainly didn't belong there. But I played the game for thirty days. Sometimes my parents came to visit me, but only when there were group sessions. I did what I had to do to get out of there. Looking back, I learned a little bit, okay a lot! It was a good mediation point for me to express to my parents how unhappy I was living in corn country. One of the most pivotal moments in my move to Pennsylvania and the depression that followed was the day I left New York. My best friend in the whole world, Cheryl was standing on our front lawn in New York for the last time, crying and waving goodbye to me. I was in the backseat of the car crying and waving goodbye to her too. I had no idea how I was going to deal without her. I've never had a best friend like her and I won't ever again. Cheryl was a beautiful blond as well and with eyes as blue as the ocean. Her and Misty could've been sisters. We went to pre-school together and grew up together. When you said my name, Cheryl's name would follow and vice versa. Our parents were the best of friends as well. To this day, her father Paul still raves about how beautiful my mother was. Our mothers were both teachers in our school system. Our families just gelled together. We would sleep over each other's house almost every weekend. We were joined at the hip for lack of better words. I had no one in Pennsylvania that ever compared to my friendship with Cheryl. She wasn't just my best friend, she was my sister. She was the other part of me and my life that was so pure and so innocent. When I think back to those days, I think nothing but happiness. Honestly, those days got me through a lot of the ups and downs of my recovery. When we moved to Pennsylvania I was hurting so much and my parents couldn't see it. Or were my 'brass balls' in full swing? No pun intended. I wanted to see Cheryl again. I wanted my friend. I wanted to share the rest of our teen years growing up together and share boyfriend stories and have slumber parties and eventually grow up, get married to the loves of our lives and have our children become best friends as well. But all I had was myself. It was only me. Cheryl and I stayed in touch briefly for about a year. When the whole slicing of the wrists happened my parents, instead of letting me call regularly, denied me access to Cheryl. I wasn't allowed to call or write to her. Mom actually intercepted the letters I was trying to sneak to the mailbox. They said it was one of the reasons I did what I did. So, instead of helping me fill the void of losing my friend, they ripped it away from me even more. I wasn't allowed to contact anyone of my friends in New York, especially Cheryl. This made me hate my parents; and hate is a very strong word. As the years went on, I'd kept all those letters I didn't mail to Cheryl only to burn them in the fire place before moving to Florida after I graduated high school. I thought I would never see her again.

Eight years later, the night my mother died, I was going through Mom's phone book contacting all the people that needed to be notified of her death. I came across Cheryl's parents old phone number in New York. Before I ran to the church to have my screaming session with God, I sat there at the kitchen table by myself while everyone was in the bedroom saying goodbye to my dead mother. The mortician was on his way to pick her up to take her to the morgue. You would've thought I would be in there saying my final goodbyes but mom took her last breath and died in my arms; I already said my goodbyes. Besides, I was about to see if I could get part of my life back that I had lost so many years ago. All I could do was stare at the phone number with my hand on the phone, remembering the last time I saw and talked to Cheryl, waving goodbye to her through the rear view window of my parents car as a 15 year old little girl. I was remembering the day I sliced my wrists. My heart started pounding in my ears and in that instant I picked up the phone and dialed the number. I got the message machine, it was Cheryl's mom on the recording. They still lived there.

"Um, hi there Mr. and Mrs. Greene. This is Christina Giordano. Wow, it's been a long time. I have some bad news. I didn't want to leave it on a message machine but here goes. My mom, Diane passed away tonight. I know Mrs. Greene that you and her were very good friends. I really hope you remember me as Cheryl and I were best friends since we were 4 years old. If you could please tell her that I never stopped being her best friend, I would appreciate it. If you could relay this to her and ask her to please call me, I would be so happy to hear from her. Thank you and good night."

I was shaking like a leaf the whole time I left that message. Would her mother give Cheryl the message? Could I get back my best friend who I lost so long ago? Would she call me? What would I say?

Two days later, after leaving the message for Cheryl's parents, I was at my dad's house sitting at the kitchen table with him preparing the arrangements for my mom's funeral. The funeral had to be made into a huge production of course. The show *had* to include all the bells and whistles because her mother, (you guys call that a grandmother but not me), had to look important and take the 'grieving mother of her only child' to the highest level of sympathy she could get. We were in the kitchen looking at a book filled with the gaudiest flower arrangements I've ever seen when the phone rang.

"Hello?", I answered thankful to get away from all the funeral arrangement stuff.

"Yeah, um. Hi, is Christina Giordano there?" When I heard the voice on the other end, I dropped to my knees with tears in my eyes.

"Yes, this is her? Cheryl? Is this you?" I knew her voice. I could never forget it. Even after eight years of not hearing it, I still knew her voice.

"Yeah girl, it's me!"

"Oh my God, Cheryl I've missed you so much!"

We were on the phone for an hour talking about the past eight years and what life held for us. By looking at the area code on her phone, she knew I lived in Florida.

"What part of Florida do you live in?", she asked.

"Marco Island, why?"

"How close is that to Cape Coral?"

"About an hour South", I responded trying to figure out what she was getting at.

"Christina, my soon to be husband went to Cape Coral High School and we will be down there next month visiting his family. No excuses, we are coming down there to see you too!", she replied.

Moved by this, I started crying, trying to keep my cool.

A month later, my Cheryl and her soon to be husband showed up at my place of work. When I saw her walking down the path to my office, I ran down the balcony stairs and sprinted across the tennis courts. I worked at a country club as the assistant tennis pro and I left 2 clients sitting on the balcony that day to run after my friend. As she started running towards me we embraced each other and held on like our lives had finally came to a completion. Those eight years were gone now and as we held on tight to each other crying, I had this overwhelming feeling that this part of my life, the depression of so many years not having her in my life was finally gone. That hurt I felt as a child was finally gone. It was like those eight years never existed. We picked right up where we left off. We told her fiancé about the last time we saw each other, the day she was standing on my front lawn in New York and me in the back seat of my parents car waving goodbye to each other. We both started getting teary eyed, looking at each other smiling all night during dinner. I thought my face was going to crack I was smiling so hard! I finally had my Cher Bear back. A few years later, she got married and moved to Cape Coral. I had decided to move there as well. We now live right down the street from each other and at the time this book is being written, we are going on forty-three years of being best friends. I never told her about slicing my wrists, though. I wanted to move forward with her without all the darkness I'd experienced. To this day, I don't think she ever knew. When she reads this book is when she'll know.

***

When I got out of the psych unit after slicing my wrists, I returned to school with serious restrictions. I wasn't allowed to hang out with my friends, I wasn't allowed to go to football games, school dances and my mom had to drive me to school every day. I was on lock down, sort of. I wanted to go to the movies with my friends one night and my parents wouldn't let me. I began to argue my point with them. They ripped me away from Cheryl and my life. They wouldn't let me call or write to her. They intercepted my letters to her. They wouldn't let me do anything except go to school, come home, do homework, eat dinner, and go to my room. I wasn't allowed to go over any of my friends' houses, they had to come to our house. They were doing exactly what the psych doctor told them not to do. They were isolating me. Especially my mother. My father had about enough of the arguing and so did I. I told both of them to go fuck themselves and ran up the stairs to my room as fast as I could. I heard my dad running after me and tried to close the door before he could get to it, but I wasn't strong enough and I wasn't fast enough to do it. He wrestled me down to the ground, but I put up a pretty good fight against a 250-pound man. But then he straddled me, locked my arms down underneath his knees and grabbed the front of my hair close to my forehead and proceeded to slam my head into the bedroom floor. He managed to knock me out but before he did, I heard my mother yell words I'll never forget.

"Stop Joe! You're going to make yourself sick!"

What the fuck! Did I just hear her right? He's going to make *himself* sick? Lady, do you not see that this crazy motherfucker is slamming your daughter's head into the floor? Then the world went black. When I came to,

I was locked in my bedroom. So what did I do? I opened the window, crawled out to the roof of the first floor and jumped off. I learned to stop, drop and roll really quick, and ran off into the pitch black night. I wasn't going to put up with being a caged animal anymore, I was out of there. They took my friends away, they ripped me away from the only people, places and things I ever knew or cared about. I tried to tell them, but they didn't listen. I tried to show them, but they locked me up and now I was getting the crap beat out of me. *Now, fuck that! I'm out!* As I ran into the night, I had only one place to go; the movies. This whole scene played a very prominent role in my choice for men in my later years. I loved my father. But he hurt me. My mother hurt me. The physical pain heals. The emotional pain doesn't, so I buried it deep down inside of me and never spoke of it again. That old saying is so wrong; 'Sticks and stones may break my bones but words can never hurt me' is a bunch of bullshit. Abuse is abuse.

***

My parents and I apologized to each other and life went on normally. But the fact that my father had the capacity to flip out like that on his own daughter was always in the back of my mind. When I got older I was stronger against him. I remember him pissing me off one night after my mother died, raising his hand to strike me in the kitchen. He had been drinking and treating my sister like Cinderella. To this day, I can't remember what was actually said but I do remember slapping him very hard across the face and telling him to snap out of his pity party and wake the fuck up because mom wasn't coming back. I think he finally realized that night that teaching me to stand up for myself early on had bit him in the ass. No daughter would ever think to smack her father across the face. Especially when she loved and admired him so much. But I did. He never raised his hand to me ever again nor did he beat me again. I think he figured it was going to be a losing battle on so many levels, and did everything he could to make it up to me. And in return, he gained my respect. When I moved in with him to take care of him after his stay in the hospital, we would always eat dinner together, break out the old 45's and listen to some of the best jazz and swing music ever recorded. We started to become friends again and enjoy the music and each other. He was sixty-three and his health was deteriorating He still enjoyed smoking cigars and hiding his perfect bourbon Manhattans from me in the cabinet in his bathroom. As long as he didn't get mean while he was drinking, why should I put any demand on him to stop. I wanted him to enjoy what he loved to do. It would only take two or three drinks for him to get hammered. When this happens, it's usually a good sign that your liver is saturated with alcohol and failing to work properly. It can't filter the alcohol anymore so it hits your blood stream faster. I didn't want to lose him, but the end was closer than I thought.

***

On February 5th, 2012, the night the New York Giants won the Super Bowl, I was.bartending in a little Italian restaurant and when I got home, I ran up the stairs so delighted that my dad's favorite team, The Giants won! But to my surprise, dad was laying on the floor.

"Dad? Dad! What happened? Are you alright? Jesus! What happened?", I said falling to my knees beside him.

"Oh Christina," he responded with slurred speech, "I think I've fallen. But the kicker is, I can't get up. I fell off the wagon a little bit."

"Ya think? Ok, let's try to get you up."

When trying to pick dead weight of 210 pounds is like trying to pick up a Chevy Escalade, it's not going to happen.

"Nope! Chrissy, I don't think we're going to get me up."

I actually sat there and put a pillow under his head and started laughing uncontrollably. Then, he started laughing and I started laughing harder. We were laughing uncontrollably, about what I have no idea! We always laughed and joked about something that could be really disturbing to others. Then all of a sudden, he stopped laughing staring up at me with tears in his eyes.

"I'm done Chrissy. I don't want to be here anymore. Twenty years without your mom is long enough. It's too painful to go on anymore. I just want to be with my Diane."

I looked directly in to my father's eyes and held his face in my hands and I said holding back my tears, "I know daddy. I know. Soon. I promise you. You'll be with her soon." Thirty-eight days later, he was gone.

***

The morning my father passed away will be one that stays with me forever. I remember every word and every movement and every moment that happened. Dad stormed into my room at 5:45 a.m. on March 14th, 2012 yelling, "Chrissy? Chrissy, wake up! I can't breathe. Something's happening!"

"Ok dad ok! Where does it hurt?", I said jumping out a bed and in total delirium. I tried to shake my head to wake up.

"Underneath my left armpit! I can't breathe Chrissy! We got to call the ambulance!"

For my father to say that I knew it was bad. I ran to the phone and called 911. I began to take dad's pulse and then felt his forehead. He felt like a clam. Hot and cold at the same time.

When the paramedics got there, which seemed like immediately, they ran upstairs and put an oxygen mask on my dad's face. I knew the captain on duty and it definitely helped. Chris was always very kind to my father and me. He asked me about his medications he was on and so forth while I kept looking away to see the what the other EMTs were doing to my father. It was 6:10 a.m. as they were strapping my father into a chair gurney to take him down the stairs. As I stood at the top of the stairs, a feeling came over me I can't explain. It was a chill of relief. Like something escaped my body.

I looked at Chris and asked, "Chris, is my dad having a heart attack?"

Chris turned slowly to me with a tears in his eyes, "Christina, I'm only a paramedic. I'm not allowed to tell you."

My mouth dropped open and I yelled down the stairs to my dad.

"Daddy! Daddy!"

He turned and looked up at me.

With tears in my eyes and pain in my heart I yelled out to him, "Daddy! I love you so much! Daddy!"

He took the oxygen mask off his face and with tears in his eyes and a slight smile on his face he said to me, "I love you too, Chrissy."

We stared at each other for what seemed like a lifetime. The paramedics took him to the hospital I grabbed his wallet and whatever else I thought they might need with me.

He died at 6:18 a.m., immediately after the ambulance drove off. I didn't know until I arrived at the hospital that he had died. I was numb. After coming home from the hospital, I sat in my dad's favorite chair and realized in that instance, I was now *completely* alone. What was going to happen now? What was I supposed to do without him? So many unanswered questions.

While sitting in his chair, the music that had left me so long ago came back to me oddly enough. I got out a pen and paper and the lyrics to one of my songs 'It's Only Me', was written that day.

When the whiskey flows from the bottle

I can feel that old familiar sting

Then he said, "Those better days are gone"

And I, I feel I'm breaking down

And I, I feel I don't know how

I can feel you in my head

A silent cry for me

I'm right where, right where I

I wanted to be

I tried for so long

To make you see

I go through all the motions now

Cause this time, It's Only Me

You gave me a voice to carry on

Now I sit here all alone

That life slipped away

And somehow I lost it all

Oh It's Only Me this time

Holding my head up high

I carry all the memories

And I'll remember the last goodbye

In my darkest dreams I scream

An illusion of only me

I'll be fine you'll see it in my eyes

Cause it's only me this time

You wrap me in your wings

When I'm about to fall

I can't hear your voice no

No I can't see you anymore

So here I am among

What used to be

I go through all the motions now

But this time It's Only Me

Oh, how I miss my dad.

CHAPTER 3

ANGELS AND DEMONS

***

Beloved, do not believe every spirit, but test the spirits to see whether they are from God, for many false prophets have gone out into the wild. ~1 John 4:1

As life goes through its ups and downs, I've learned a few lessons. One particular lesson I learned from my father was not to trust anyone and the more money you have, the happier you are. I would soon find out that the later part of that lesson is false and the beginning part of that lesson I never learned. At thirty years old, I was told I had three fibroid tumors on my uterus that would inhibit me from having children. They were the size of small chicken eggs. I was also diagnosed with the same low blood platelet disease as my mother had and was also diagnosed with severe anemia. I got a triple whammy all in one trip to the doctor's office and subsequently I had no choice but to accept the fact that I wasn't able to have children. But the Gods' honest truth is this; I never wanted to bring a child into this fucked up world of mine. Honestly, I think I would have been a terrible mother. I could barely take care of myself even though I was straight, clean and sober at the time. I suppose I was a little selfish as well. I didn't like kids. They got on my nerves. I look back now and it wasn't so much that I disliked them - I envied them. I saw the potential in children around me and felt they had a way better chance to follow their dreams. They had the chance to live their lives exactly the way they wanted to, but I couldn't. My dreams and hopes always seemed to get smashed because I was always taking care of everyone else. But to my surprise, I got pregnant right before my ex-husband Brandon and I got married. We both decided it wasn't the right time to have a kid. We were too young and two weeks away from getting married when we found out. Our whole lives were still ahead of us. I had the abortion right after we got back from our honeymoon in Bermuda. The abortion didn't faze me as much as it does other people. Some people never forgive themselves for it. I was different. Maybe I should be remorseful in some people's eyes, but it never really played any important role in my life. I had way too much going for me and I didn't want the burden of being tied down to a child. Changing diapers and getting my hands full of piss and shit wasn't my idea of a grand 'ole time. However, when it comes to animals, I have the softest heart and I don't mind potty training dogs. They don't cry and they obey, unlike most human trolls I've ever come in contact with. I just never liked kids. I had and do have absolutely no patience whatsoever for offspring. But it delights me when a puppy learns a new trick.

***

Animals, whether they are dogs, cats, horses, chickens, fishes or lions have a survival instinct other animals don't. Some are flight animals, running away from any threatening situation and some animals are fight animals. But when you look into their eyes, they tell the story of where they came from, where they've been and where they are. They don't lie to you. They love you unconditionally, they look up to you, you are their leader and you are their family. They love you until their last breath. I found I could understand an animal better than any human, and they in turn could understand me especially when I couldn't understand myself.

I've always wanted a horse. For some reason those fifteen hundred pound animals intrigued me. How do people control an enormous creature like that? I wanted to know. I wanted to feel what it was like to run a horse at top speed. I wanted to fly. Then one day in 1997, a beautiful ten-year-old dark bay thoroughbred horse named Creed came into my life. Creed's grandsire was Man O'War. You might remember him as one of the greatest racehorses of all time. Man O'War won twenty-one out of his twenty-two career races. Creed was fast. At a top speed clocked at 45 miles per hour, Creed flew like the wind. Creed was the spitting image of his grandsire; 16.2 hands high and dark bay from muzzle to tail. Creed was the most majestic horse I'd ever seen in my life. He stood tall and proud every time I was on his back. I was enough for him and he was enough for me. He filled every void in my heart I ever had and he mended every wound in my soul. I gave him everything that was left of me at that time and Creed always gave me 100% of his spirit. But now, he needed to be king of his own barn because that is what he deserved. In 1998, my father gave me the down payment to buy some land to build a house and barn on. I suppose the guilt of beating me when I was young and the fact that I gave up my dream as a musician so my sister could go to college and do absolutely nothing with the degree she received, weighed heavy on him. When the farm was completed in January of 1999, Creed and I moved in. I'd rescued an Egyptian Arabian foal that was orphaned too, so Creed had some company in the barn. Creed was a gentle soul. I had been reading up on different riding disciplines and was told that he was trained in *English Style* discipline but would ride as a western horse as well. With the help of a friend, I mounted in my new saddle that I had custom made specifically to Creeds back and measurements. That damn saddle cost me $3000 dollars! Within 2 weeks we were riding together like we were one. I could think of moving left and he would immediately on queue pick up a left lead. Creed read my mind like no other creature, human or otherwise, could do. I'd never felt so in tune with something before that day. Looking back now and the twelve years we shared together, Creed was by far one of the greatest things in my life. He was the one thing I got right. During those twelve years, Creed was always there for me. We shared a lot with each other. In times of good and bad, he was always my sanity. Then one day after I got home from work I went down to the barn to feed him and found him lying in the pasture dead. I ran beside him, dropped to my knees screaming. My best friend, my confidant, my beloved horse was gone. The one thing that gave me a reason to live was gone. I slept in the pasture that night curled up between his front hooves. When I woke up the next morning cradled against my dead horse's chest I gave him a final kiss, cut off his mane with my knife and called the vet to have him picked up and buried. I still have his mane hair to this day, tucked away in my dresser drawer. His spirit will always be with me. He will always be the one thing I got right in my life.

My other best friend was a border collie named Dusty. I watched Dusty being born on April 22, 2002 in my barn. He was the product of my purebred border collie, Duke and my neighbors' pit bull. He was darn handsome! After 64 days of gestation, I became a grandma! Dusty was as good as a herder as Duke was and they both tormented Creed. That horse was smart though, he knew exactly what was going to happen when Duke and Dusty came running full speed ahead out to the pasture. Creed would take a deep breath and play the game of the two herding dogs nipping at a horse's hooves. For five years I had a pretty simple and easygoing life. It was a good life. Nobody bothered me. These animals were my 'kids'. But then one day, a demon entered my life disguised as an elevator man. His name was Larry.

**

I met Larry at work. We both worked for West Coast Elevator Company in Naples, Florida. He took a liking to me and me being little miss independent, didn't give him the time of day at first. In the years to come, I should've stuck to my guns. I mean what was I thinking? I had a good simple life. I had my own five-acre horse ranch. Nobody told me what to do or where to go. I'd made it man! I suppose I was just missing one thing, someone to share it with. It had been five years since I was with anyone, sexually or relationship wise. I was craving companionship other than two dogs and a horse. I finally gave in to Larry's advances and started dating him. After ninety days, he gave me a promise ring. Ninety days after that he gave me an engagement ring. Ninety days after that I married him and ninety days after marrying him, he started beating the shit out of me. See a pattern here? I guess some of my not feeling good enough definitely started with my father beating me. I think I equated this to love. He was a full-blown alcoholic just like my dad but a nasty, violent one at that. Oh, the irony. To this day, I hate Johnny Cash. When Larry would beat me senseless and leave me withering on the living room floor in pain and in my own blood, he would pop in Johnny Cash's Greatest Hits and play Folsom Prison Blues or Ring of Fire blaring loud to the point the windows would shake. I managed to keep my family out of the picture. It was quite easy because Larry isolated me from everyone and everything. I was a prisoner in my own home. I could go to work and come home and that was it. The only thing I was good for was being a punching bag and an object to rape every night. When he was done with me, he would pass out giving me the time to crawl out of bed and go to the barn with Duke and Dusty. The three of us would hide in Creeds stall. Duke and Dusty would lick my wounds and comfort me and Creed would lay down with us and keep us safe. I would look up to the sky and pray. I didn't know who I was praying to but I was praying. I would often pray to die. But then I would look at Duke, Dusty and Creed and think, 'what would happen to them if I died?' No, I had to live for them. For my three boys. So, I endured more. One night, he broke the cartilage in my nose causing it to bleed all over the floor. He made me lick the blood up until the floor was clean. If I stopped for one second he would grab my ponytail and shove my face into the blood on the tile floor. He was a monster. He was every demon that ever was all put into one human. I accepted that this is what was going to be the rest of my life. Being raped every night, made to lick my own blood off the floor, and being tormented with a loaded shotgun. He used to walk around the house with a Katana strapped to him. A Katana is an oriental sword. It has a 3ft blade on it and the tang, which is the handle, is balanced to be swung with one hand. I can't even count how many times I felt the breeze of that blade being swung at my face. Life as I knew it had ended. This was my fate. This was Karma. What had I done to deserve this most excruciating abuse? I was living in fear of my life every day. Thank God I knew I couldn't have children. As many time's as Larry raped me over and over again, I thanked God every time that I was sterile. After a while it was routine. I would get dragged into the bedroom, smacked around and then raped. I grew expressionless. I had no choice but to lay there because there was nothing I could do. Larry was smart even though he was a drunk. He'd always lock Dusty and Duke out because they would growl and lunge at him. Dusty was half Pitbull. It's not a good idea to make a Pitbull angry. Then it finally happened; Larry forgot to lock Dusty and Duke out.

As was routine, he would grab me by the hair, beat me around until I was too tired to fight back, dragging me into the bedroom for my nightly raping. It was early evening as the sun had just started to set, I saw Dusty out the corner of my eye, teeth bared and his fur standing on end. Dusty had the fur of a border collie but the muscle mass of a Pitbull. Growling and running towards us he looked like a werewolf. I'd never seen a crazed look on an animal as I saw in Dusty that night. He made his way fiercely across the living room and through the threshold of the bedroom. In a split second as Larry lifted me up by my neck with both of his hands and threw me on the bed choking me, my werewolf jumped on Larry's back and grabbed a hold of him by the nape of his neck and bit down. Larry was now on the floor trying to fend Dusty off in his drunken state, as the blood curdling growling commenced.

"Christina! Call him off! Call him off!" squealing like the pig that he was.

I replied laughing hysterically, "Call him off yourself you piece of no good shit!"

***

He was no match for Dusty, especially drunk as he was, and I was free. I immediately went to the phone and dialed 911. Living out in the woods it takes a little while for the officers to get there. I ran out of the house as Dusty was keeping a squealing Larry at bay and bloody. I called Duke to run out the door with me then it was time to get Dusty. After yelling frantically to my beautiful savior to come, Dusty finally snapped out of his crazed mind and let Larry go. The three of us jumped in the truck and headed to the neighbor's house. Wendy was a great friend and great neighbor. We had our differences sometimes, but all friends do. She was a tiny spitfire of a girl and a bit more materialistic then me, but I tried not to judge her for it. She hated Larry and every chance she had she would let him know it. She was there for me in a desolate time and I thank her for keeping my boys and me safe that day. Wendy was dating the son of the Florida State Attorney at the time and they both just happened to be fixing the front fence at her house when I drove up. Wendy was outside also.

"What's wrong? You're white as a ghost! What did he do to you?" Wendy knew everything since the first day he beat me up until then. I always confided in her.

"Wendy, I can't go home! He's going to kill me!" I said crying and shaking. I was an absolute mess. I was covered in Larry's blood from Dusty as I jumped out of the truck.

"Holy shit! What the fuck did he do to you?"

"Don't worry, it's not my blood, it's his! Dusty ripped him apart! I have to hide Dusty and Duke. The cops are coming!" I said frantically.

"Ok, I'll take them back to my barn. You go inside and wash the blood off and put a change of my clothes on! And for Christ sake, be quick about it!"

Wendy and her boyfriend hid Dusty and Duke in her barn. Larry would for sure tell the officers that Dusty was a Pitbull and that would ensure Dusty's fate to be euthanized after an attack like that. I wasn't about to have my hero put to sleep.

***

As I washed the blood off and changed my clothes, the State Attorney was waiting for the cops to arrive. Wendy called the police and notified them that I was at her house. The officers showed up after they went and talked to Larry. Larry had been arrested and taken into custody. I never saw him again after June 22, 2007. I've spent every day for three and a half years of my life getting beaten and raped endlessly. I was finally free from the nightmare of what I thought was going to be the rest of my life. I had been waiting patiently for the perfect time to get away. I had to make sure that if I ever did get away, there would be no way of him coming back to complete the task of killing me. Larry would have done it. In my heart and my soul, if it wasn't for this day happening, it would not have been long before he would've taken my life. Larry was brought up on charges of domestic violence, battery, kidnapping and assault with a deadly weapon without intent to kill. I managed with the help of the State Attorney's office to lock him up in State Prison for five years and during his stay, I divorced him. This is when my Uncle Joe Gambino took over. Larry got out of prison in 2011 and I believe his kneecaps are somewhere in that prison. I suppose that taught him a lesson. He never came looking for me again. Duke died a year and a half later. I lost the ranch 6 months after I went to live with my father. Dusty came with me and lived out the rest of his natural life as my hero and my savior. I'll never forget that he saved my life. He was my constant companion, my confidant and he had my heart for fifteen years. There will never be another dog like him. His actual footprint is tattooed on my right upper arm and simply reads "Dusty". There is a lesson to be learned in every stage your life. Never lose sight of your passions. Things that make you elated to be alive are the things that keep you alive and sometimes save your life. I've now come to recognize the difference between angels and demons. Demons are very easily disguised and sometimes angels are too. Neither angels nor demons have any prejudice. And the wrath of an angel can destroy a demon whether real or living inside of you. Pay attention to the messages because there is one hidden in every angel and every demon, yet both creatures teach you a lesson.

CHAPTER 4

THE BEGINNING

***

She is clothed in strength and dignity and she laughs without fear of the future.
~ Proverbs 31:25

Sometimes, when the shit hits the fan, you simply need to wipe that crap off your ass and move on. That's what I realized after the whole Larry experience. I look back now and maybe I should've sought some counseling for that. He played a vital part in my future relationships with men and people in general. I had once again vowed to never let anyone or anything control me or my life like that again. Who would've thought that a substance could destroy me just as much as Larry did? New Year's Eve, 2010 was the highlight of the year for me. My friends and I went to a local hangout called 'CJ's on the Bay' in Marco Island to party. When the clock struck midnight, I was propped up against the fountain in the courtyard trying desperately not to fall over while watching everyone kiss their significant others. I'd never spent a New Year's Eve with anyone. To this day I've never experienced a New Year's Eve kiss, at least not a genuine one. I suppose someday I will know what that feels like, but this particular year was no different than the rest. Well, not really. From what I remembered I looked pretty hot that night, decked out in heels and a tight black dress. But that didn't cover up the fact that by midnight, I was walking like Bambi on ice. I don't know what came over me that night. I think watching everyone around me kissing made me jealous. No one was paying attention to *me*. I hated being invisible in a room. I always had something to show the world. I wanted people to hear my music, not that any of these people had any idea I had a voice, I just needed the attention.

I took my heels off and climbed to the top of the fountain in the middle of the courtyard. I stood tall and proud up there at the top looking down at the little people below me like they were my lowly subjects. To me, they were small and insignificant. They meant nothing to me. Yet, I wanted them to see me. So, I belted out the most spectacular version of the *National Anthem* they had ever heard aside from Whitney Houston at the time. As I started to sing, the echo of my voice carried throughout the courtyard and across Marco Bay. People stopped wishing each other a Happy New Year and stopped sucking each other's faces and turned to *me*. They were all listening *me* sing in total amazement. As I hit that infamous high note towards the end of the song, everyone started cheering, whistling and yelling, 'Bravo'! Finally, they saw *me*. I was where I wanted to be that night, the center of attention. It felt amazing to command the attention of three hundred people I didn't know, and to boot, they loved me! All while standing on the top of a fountain, smashed on New Year's Eve. Quite a few famous people live on Marco Island. There was an older man there named Sam. He was supposedly the director of the *National Hockey League Network* as that was the way he introduced himself to me as he graciously helped me off the fountain after I sang. He offered to buy me a drink so we headed to the bar. Far be it for me to say no to a free cocktail, besides, all the guys were eyeing me now anyway. I had my pick of whoever I wanted to take to the sack that night. I finally got the attention I was craving. After hearing me sing, who wouldn't want to be with a talented, pretty woman like me. Unfortunately, beauty is only skin deep. I was angry, needy and ugly on the inside. I figured Sam only wanted to get his hand under my dress so I played the little game with him. He wasn't my type at all. He was old and fat. I liked good looking bad boys, the kind of guys that make your panties wet. You know what I'm talking about. The ones that look at you like they are undressing you with their eyes. They *must* have a great body and be an animal in bed. But for some reason, the good looking bad boys never came on to me. It was always the older men. Then you see these big girls with four teeth in their mouth getting picked up by four guys as soon as she steps foot in a bar and you think to yourself, "What the hell does that cow have over me?" Therein lies the ugliness in a person. Those girls were probably sweet as honey inside with a heart of gold, unlike mine at the time. I look back on how I was and can't believe that was me.

Sam preceded to tell me what he did for a living and that he was a big somebody. Looking back now, it kind of makes me laugh because I found out later he was the animal mascot for a farm league team. But he did get me into the *Florida Everblades Hockey League* as one of their main Anthem singers. I spent six seasons singing for them and they loved me as much as I loved them. I contacted major league baseball and hockey teams to see if I could sing for them too. I didn't owe anything to an old wannabe trying to get in my pants so after I used Sam for what I needed, I moved on and forgot about him. Then, one day I got a call from the commissioner of the *East Coast National Hockey League*. He offered me the honor of singing the

National Anthem at *Madison Square Garden* for *The New York Rangers*! Holy shit Batman! I'm going to sing at Madison Square Garden! This was an unbelievable opportunity. To sing Acapella in front of eighteen thousand people! That doesn't happen to people like me! But it was happening. I was scheduled for the March 17th game against the *Pittsburgh Penguins*. I got two seats at the game, a plane flight and hotel room. I thought of only one person good enough to be by my side that night, my dad. Two weeks before we were supposed to fly to New York, we made a quick stop in Tampa so I could sing the National Anthem for the *New York Yankees* spring training game against the *Minnesota Twins*. Dad liked that game. He loved the New York Yankees. We had so much fun together that day, just me and him. I sang the National Anthem better than anytime I had in the past; better than the night I climbed to the top of the fountain in that courtyard. On the way home from Tampa that day, my dad kept telling me how proud he was of me.

"You nailed the shit out of that Anthem today kid!"

"Yeah? I did? Thanks, dad. It felt good coming out. I was perfectly on pitch, wasn't I?"

"As perfect as perfect could be. The timber, pitch and key were absolutely exquisite!"

I'm glad I impressed my dad so much that day. Nothing felt better to me than my dad being proud of me. It was a big deal. He wound up passing away that next week and never got to go to Madison Square Garden with me. I went alone and sang in honor of him that night. As I hit the last note, I pointed straight up to heaven. That was for you daddy. After dad died, I finally had the chance to live my life for myself. However, I was a forty-two-year-old washed up wannabe musician. I was too old for the music industry to even look at me now. There I was with no dreams left. No ambition to do anything except write lyrics to songs that would never be recorded and be labeled as *'The National Anthem Singer of Marco Island'*. If you needed the Anthem sung, call Christina. Wow, what an honor! I was a one hit wonder. I still played my flute and violin every day. Such sad music came out of my instruments. Always playing in the key of E minor. Think of your Tim Burton music from *'A Nightmare Before Christmas'*, *'Lord of The Rings'* soundtracks or *'Harry Potter'*. All those soundtracks are written in E Minor. That beautifully sad music that tells a tale of sorrow and despair. That's the only music that came out of me anymore. All I had left was my dismal music and no one to play it to.

***

A few months passed when I found out my friend Johnny was desperate for a lead singer for his band, *Tantrum*. It was a perfectly named band for Johnny to be the leader of because he was the epitome of a tantrum, a temper tantrum. He was always nice to me, but to other people he was a tyrant. It was fun and even though I wasn't rich and famous, it filled the void in me where my dreams once resided. But I wanted the world to hear *my* words. *My* lyrics to *my* songs. The band eventually broke up because of an overly angered and drunken Johnny and a guitarist named Gary whose ego was so big his head couldn't fit through a standard front door. So, I decided to put together a band that I could write music for my lyrics. But I wasn't going to find that kind of talent in Marco Island, Florida. They were a bunch of has-been musicians. In their minds, a good night was playing *Mustang Sally* in front of fifty and sixty-year-old people at the *Moose Lodge* and to add to the misery, the pay for the night was a spaghetti dinner. I needed real talent, musicians and not a spaghetti dinner! I'm Italian, for god sakes! I can make my own spaghetti dinner and a much better one too! I'd heard about the local original music scene in Cape Coral, Florida. It was a about an hour north of Marcos Island where amazing musicians where waiting to be heard and the bonus was that my best friend Cheryl lived there. The talent that poured out of the scene there was on par to New York's Greenwich Village, from what I understood. So, I started friending some people in the music scene on Facebook and eventually found out that a good friend of mine Denise, who was well known to everyone there, photographed the bands. I tagged along with her to a club one night called, *The Buddha Lounge*. It was my first show I saw in that area. A well-known band from Indiana called, *Losing September* was headlining the show. They got their name from the downfall of my beautiful home town city of New York. It was a play on words in reference to the terrorist attacks on 9/11 when my city fell from the sky. I'd heard them play on *YouTube* before and found their music enjoyable. Besides, the lead singer was classically trained as I was in voice and instruments, plus he sang opera as well. When one trains as a vocalist who can also scream heavy metal rock music at the top of their lungs *and* still be in key and perfect pitch, you've got one hell of a talented singer. When you choose to be a musician and you go to watch other musicians play, it's hard to have a good time. My father always said, *"A tin ear can't hear"*. This means that non-trained musicians can't hear the very painful pitches and tones that trained musicians can. I'm good at hearing these mistakes, so much so, I can tell when a drummer forgets one stick stroke. Sometimes that's good and sometimes it's bad.

***

There were two other bands playing that night, *'Before the Fire'* and *'10-Even'*, who were both local hard hitting popular bands and I guess you could say local celebrities. I wanted to see both of those bands as Denise spoke very highly of them so I was eager to see them perform. Cape Coral seemingly was spewing raw talent into the scene. *10-Even* was the first band to perform. As the lights came up, the music started and there he was, Matt, playing lead guitar. Matt was a talented musician. One of the most incredible guitar players I'd ever seen. I was mesmerized by him and his music. The sound Matt brought to my ears was undeniably the most raw, hard, classical, tasty music I'd heard in a long time. And he was unbelievably sexy. He sported a blond Mohawk on his head, ripped up jeans that matched his ripped up shirt. He was fit and muscular. He definitely had a little bad boy image going on. It was like watching someone fuck a guitar in public. That guitar was completely submissive to Matt. It was like watching a sex scene from a great porn flick. I turned to the guy standing next to me and said,

"Holy shit! That guy is a phenomenal on that lead guitar!"

"Yeah! That's Matt, he's sick!", yelling his response.

"Matt, huh? That's his name? Well, I'm going to fuck that and make it mine one day. That you can bet your nuts on." Yeah, I was sick in lust with Matt.

***

Three more months went by and I made good on my statement. I did the dirty deed and made him mine.

Matt and I started dating in December of 2013. It started out as a one night stand but then evolved into something much deeper. Matt supported my music and during this time I found some pretty good musicians, per my standards. Honestly, there was only one I found and his name was Chad Holbrook. Chad was a kick ass guitar player and still is to this day. I got very close with him, his wife and kids. They are still a very important part of my life to this day. I nicknamed Chad my "Jiminy Cricket" because he was my so-called conscience. He always had the most magical way of talking logic into me and we could write the most bad – ass music and lyrics together. One specific day holds a closeness to my heart. While driving to band rehearsal on 9/11, I was feeling overwhelmingly somber that day, as were millions of others. I had also lost a family member and a close high school friend when the towers in New York City came crumbling down. This vision came over me of wondering if they rose up to heaven after falling to their deaths? Were they lost spiritually like I was? I mean, did they believe in God and were saved at that moment? If I had been in the towers, would anyone remember me? If I died, who would care? My parents were dead, so who would care in the end? Lyrics immediately started flooding my head. I recorded every word on my phone. When I got to band rehearsal, I ran over to Chad and said excitedly, "Dude, I have these sick lyrics I was just recording on the way up here!".

"Oh yeah? Let's hear it."

"Wait a minute, I have to write them out. Oh yeah, and I'm hearing this kind of melody with some very intense ambient sound."

All I had to do was hum a few bars and Chad knew exactly what I wanted. It's so awesome when you have a phenomenal musician like that working with you, they write to your voice. They know what is in your head and consequently what you want to hear. Others, like the rest of that band we were in, write what they wanted and then you're supposed to figure out what the hell kind of lyrics to go with the ridiculous mess they created. That my friends is what we classically trained people consider musical suicide. When you create a mess of noise that has no rhyme or reason to it. It becomes audible chaos. That day, it took Chad and I approximately 20 minutes to have the rough draft written of was to be our first recorded single, '*We the People*'. I was so proud of that song because it was the first time I felt like I achieved one of my goals. I finally wrote lyrics that were going to be heard. It may not have been the greatest song, but to me, it was one of my life dreams finally coming to fruition. The music that Chad wrote for it was fantastic. I was so proud of it and the best part was we did it together. Me and my "Jiminy Cricket".

In the end

There's no truth, no alibi

I've known regret

Shadowed by a thousand lies

Can you see them spread their wings?

Holding their head up high

A blinding light as they fly

Stand up and fight

We the People

Divided we fall

United we stand

We will hold our ground

We the People

Divided we fall

United we stand

We will hold our ground

Can you see them spread their wings?

As they soar from beneath the ashes

In this modern-day apocalypse

You'll never see the fear in their eyes

They don't believe all your lies

We stand up and tell the truth

Cause We the People

We the People are bulletproof

They cast you down from heaven

Leave you alone in hell

A sacred crime of passion

Their story they won't tell

On the graves of the ones remembered

With their names cast in stone

On the wings of the fallen angels

They will rise alone

Every anniversary of 9/11, I post the recording of '*We the People*' on my Facebook page. I'm proud of it. It's probably the only time in my life that the world will ever hear my voice recorded. I think of it as a legacy. I don't have any children but I do have friends that will hear it when I'm dead and gone and they will remember me. Like I said, it wasn't the greatest song, but it was mine and I was proud of it and I still am.

***

The name of our band was *Impact Event* and it was a great concept. It was a theatrical production set to music. Kind of like a rock opera. It told a fantastic tale of a girl named Krystina who set out to save the world from the evil that encompassed it. She created an army of five that stood by her and followed her as their leader. She led the rebels of the world into a war against the governments' ruthless military. Unfortunately, just as Krystina was on the brink of defeating the evil in the world, the military captured her and held her prisoner. How ironic this story line is now. I look back and the next year of my life played out exactly like that scenario. We never finished the story due to the band breaking up after just two performances. Chad

had neck surgery and couldn't play like he wanted to and moved his family to Kentucky. I stayed with the band after losing my Jiminy Cricket but it wasn't the same. I lost my music to my lyrics. I had so many more lyrics to sing and record but again, God took away what I loved. He took my music away from me again and once again, I had nothing. The rest of the guys started writing hard scream metal music that was trash and I finally gave up. I threw my hands up to God and said, "You win mother fucker. I'm done" and I didn't have anything to do with music ever again. But I had Matt and well, I supported him, his music, his ego and his bad habits. I was once again in for the ride of my life. He was on his way to becoming my favorite mistake.

CHAPTER 5

I LOVE THE WAY YOU HATE ME

***

Truthful words stand the test of time, but lies are soon exposed. ~*Proverbs 12:19*

Mark twain once said, "The definition of insanity is making the same mistake over and over again and expecting different results." Well, call me insane then because that's what I did. I kept making the same mistake again and again and it always got me hurt. Everyone has a need to feel loved. We all want to have that special bond with someone and sometimes it's for all the wrong reasons. Sometimes, we crave it so badly that it ruins our self-esteem then we subconsciously think that it's as good as we're going to get or deserve. I say bullshit to that now, but there was a time when I loved so hard I was blinded by my emotions.

Matt was my favorite mistake. I used to say that jokingly to him when deep inside I knew he was just a big fat mistake in general. After the first night, I saw him on stage I was on a mission to fuck him and own him. I completed that mission, no problem and then worked on my next quest with him. I moved to Cape Coral, Florida to be part of the music scene and to be closer to Matt. After all, he loved me and I loved him and we were having a fantastic time together. There was no way in hell anyone was going to take anything away from me ever again. I became ugly inside and sought out to destroy anyone in my path that tried to hurt me or take away my façade of happiness.

After I quit the band *Impact Event*, I set out on a mission to destroy then as a unit. I felt disrespected as its leader and lyricist. I started that band and it made me finally feel good about myself and the fact that people were hearing my music. I would be damned if anybody else would have what I worked for. I poured my sweat, tears and money into that band and I was stabbed in the back once again by people I had trusted like family. When you have band members, they become your family. It's like you are a team and you work together to create an art form that is uniquely your own. These guys though, well they were anything but family. They hired a new female vocalist named Roxie, whom I hated almost instantly without even knowing her. I tried to sabotage every show of theirs. I made sure they lost the battle of the bands, I made sure they would eventually dissipate. I got really good at hurting people, but mostly myself. People hated me and I absolutely loved it. The more they hated me the better I felt. I thought I was in control of their emotions, but in actuality, I was out of control of my own. I was a woman scorned and wasn't going to stop at anything to blast your name out there and drag you through the dirt. I had hurt enough in my life. It was time for everyone else to hurt. The brick wall I built up around me was 3 feet thick, you couldn't touch me and there was no way you were getting through it. *Impact Event* eventually fizzled out, with Roxie quitting the band right before that happened. She messaged me one day and we talked, hashed everything out and became very good friends ironically.

She's actually my hair dresser now and has seen me many times messed up beyond recognition. She still to this day has never judged me through any of it. There are people that come into your life for a reason. Roxie came into mine to show me how to forgive, not to judge and how to be kind again. Lord knows she had her hands full with me being on a three-day binge and trying to keep me from falling out of her chair while she was trying to cut my hair. That was a chore in itself. We should always forgive but never forget. As soon as we forget, we start to retrace our old steps. After I swore off music, I put all my energy into Matt. I was jealous of any woman he talked to, looked at, commented on or smiled at. Of course, he cheated on me and lied all the time which didn't help either. I always had my suspicions about him but I shook it off, as it was too difficult to believe. My insecurity was so deep that I was terrified God was going to take him from me too. I was so blinded by my emotions that it ultimately destroyed me. One can forgive just so much and so often until you no longer trust. I couldn't and still can't imagine not trusting. What a horrible way to live. For me, it makes it that much easier for the person you love to hurt you. Then as time goes on, you get used to it so it becomes routine in your life to hurt every day. Nothing changes. You just constantly live in darkness in the hope of seeing just one ray of light someday. I suppose my worst fear in life at that time was dying alone. Matt did all the right things like always being there when I needed him, putting on that façade of love and caring while sleeping with this whore or that groupie.

***

I remember one time very vividly. When I was diagnosed with tumors in my uterus in 2004, I was supposed to have a hysterectomy. At 34 years old, insurance wouldn't pay for it at the time because even though I was sterile and couldn't have children they said I was too young, and just in case I wanted to have children. That made no sense to me at all as I really can't have children, but needless to say there was no way I could afford a forty-five-thousand-dollar operation. So, I was put on medication to keep the tumors small, then my insurance finally ran out and I couldn't afford the medication. So, for 11 years I suffered the most horrible periods and eventually became anemic from losing so much blood each month. Most women dread their periods each month because of the pain. Mine were like a bloody horror film. Eventually the tumors grew so big that they started impairing my other organs. By the time 2015 rolled around I had eight tumors. Four were inside my uterus as big as grapefruits and four were growing on the outside of my uterus. Three of them were the size of oranges, putting pressure on my bladder and crushing my liver. The one that was the size of a cantaloupe was underneath my rib cage putting pressure against my lungs so much so I was having trouble breathing. I was in incredible pain all the time even when I wasn't bleeding. Matt tried to comfort my pain but was visually getting very tired of it. He was and still is an alcoholic. He was very cruel when he drank. It seems at this point you're thinking I like it! After all, my ex-husband was the same as Matt! Well, I didn't like it at all but it seems that I felt it was what I deserved. He was so violent that he'd destroy the furniture in my apartment. He broke an antique table of mine that had been in my family for over a hundred years while I was working one night. So, when I walked in, I noticed he left his anniversary Stratocaster guitar out and decided to destroy it. With great pleasure, I slammed it onto the tile floor, breaking the neck and cracking the entire guitar into pieces. Matt was passed out while all of this happened. I'm amazed he didn't hear me doing this! I left it out for him to see the next morning, nonetheless. When Matt came too, he had no recollection of breaking my antique table so I lead him to believe he destroyed his guitar as well. I never told him the truth. If he ever reads this book, he'll know then the truth of what happened that night if he doesn't already. He also raised his hand to me once. He knew about how Larry hurt me in the past and caught himself before he swung. He never remembered that either, or so he says. The stress of trying to keep tabs on Matt, wondering all the time who he was cheating on me with, was starting to add to the miserable state I was in health wise. Consequently, the results of my stress finally showed.

I came home from work on October 24, 2015 after feeling miserable at work. My period suddenly stopped after 2 weeks of bleeding like a stuck pig. When I got home and stepped out of my car, blood started pouring out of me like a water faucet, filling up my shoes. I got so lightheaded I fell to my knees in the parking lot at my apartment but managed to get myself to the front door leaving a river of blood in my wake. As I held onto the walls trying to make my way to the bathroom as quickly as possible, my hands left smears of blood on the walls. The trail of blood continued following me throughout the house. I finally made it to the bathroom and stripped off my bloody clothes, which were soaked all the way up my back from the pressure of the explosion in the parking lot. It was one of the most horrific things I had ever seen. The blood just kept pouring out of me and it wouldn't stop. I sat in the bathroom on the toilet and called Matt. I was so frightened that I was going to die. I couldn't even walk. "Matt, it's me! You have to come and get me. I just had an enormous amount of blood just explode out of me. I don't know what's happening but I think I need to go to the emergency room!", I said before he could even get a word in when he answered the phone.

"Ok", he said in a calm manner, "just hang on. I'm on my way"

Matt knew I was just like my dad in the fact that I didn't like hospitals. Something had to be pretty bad if I was saying I needed to go to the emergency room. Matt was at band rehearsal when I called so it took him about twenty minutes to get there, but when he walked into the house to get me he was horrified. I could see it in his eyes when he saw me sitting in the bathroom naked and crying in a pool of my own blood.

"Holy shit! Ok, let's get you cleaned up and put some clothes on you."

"Oh Matt, I'm so sorry. I'm sorry I'm such a burden",

He put a towel between my legs and tried frantically to clean me up and get clothes on me. We were racing against an ever-flowing river of blood. He carried me out to the car and he instantly turned into Mario Andretti to get me to the hospital before I died. Yes, it was that bad. Then, if you can believe this, they made us wait *four* hours to get treated. I was still bleeding all over the waiting room, and they made me wait? I finally made a scene because people were looking at me so I finally started yelling for immediate help.

"Can you people please do something with me? I'm hemorrhaging all over the floor here in your waiting room! Please take me back there and make me better! I don't want to die!"

Well now, that got everyone's attention really quick. Once again, even while bleeding to death, I was commanding an audience, but this time I truly felt I was going to die. With that, they took me back and ran every test imaginable. They even tried to give me a vaginal ultra sound! Good try kid! That isn't happening! The test results revealed that I had lost a pint and a half of blood. My hemoglobin was at 7.8. A normal healthy person would be at 14.0-16.0. My blood pressure was low and I was still bleeding. It was a total of seven hours of bleeding time in the hospital and I was thoroughly exhausted. Finally, they gave me a pill to stop the bleeding and sent me on my way. Really? That's it? Oh, fuck no! I got insurance now, I'm getting this taken care of! And that's exactly what I did. Three weeks later, I finally had the hysterectomy, while Matt took care of my house. I was in the hospital for a while and when I returned home, I had a sneaky suspicion he was cheating on me and to make matters more disgusting, with a fucking groupie and in *our* bed. I was right. I came home to both sides of the bed turned down like two people had slept there and long black hair on my pillow; mines shorter and brown.

***

I remember the night I found out he was cheating on me with Crisita. It was on December 21, 2015. We were watching a movie I'll never forget; it was *The Revenant* with Leonardo DiCaprio. Matt went to bed early and I finished watching the movie. We always streamed the new releases from his computer. I was about to shut down his computer when the message bar came up with a message from Crisita. Crisita was an emaciated horrid looking little creature that had no idea that make up was supposed to enhance your features, not make you look like a clown at the circus. Curious, I clicked on it. It brought me right up to his messenger app on Facebook and the message read "Hi babe. Did you tell her yet?" I didn't respond, I just kept scrolling up. I read the whole conversations from the time they met until the recent one that night. I was heartbroken. I felt sad. I felt depressed. I felt disrespected. But most of all, I felt I wasn't enough, *again*. Having a hysterectomy is incredibly serious business. The hormonal changes alone were devastating. It was like I was a totally different person. I immediately got happy again after the surgery. Matt wasn't prepared for the turn my attitude and happiness was going to take after I had my surgery. I wasn't in pain anymore. But that happiness only lasted a few weeks.

I took a screenshot of the whole conversation from Matt's computer. At the time, I didn't know why I saved it, but as I write this chapter, I now know why I did. Here's how the conversation went and I must say that when you read something like this in black and white after having your suspicions, it's one of the most hurtful things in the world. But you can be the judge of that. The conversation between Matt and Crisita that you are about to read took place On November 8, 2015. Ten days before I went to the hospital.

Matt: Hey.

Crisita: Hey

Matt: Do you have the other key to the room?

Crisita: No babe, I left it on the nightstand.

Matt: Where did you go?

Crisita: I told you I couldn't sleep. The bed was uncomfortable and you stopped holding me.

Matt: Oh, I'm sorry.

Crisita: No, don't be sorry babe. How did you sleep?

Matt: Ok, I guess.

Crisita: What are you doing for the rest of the day?

Matt: Fucking you. I have the room until 11am, would you be able to come back to the hotel room and ride me after you're done tutoring?

Crisita: Yes, love, I can do that.

This made me sick to my stomach. I just had surgery to remove twenty pounds of tumors and was skinny and beautiful again. Why didn't he want me? Why wasn't I enough? More importantly, why the fuck did I still want him? To turn the knife in my back even deeper for this sorry excuse for a woman, she had the audacity to shake my hand and introduce herself to me at Matt's show a week before! I contacted her on FB messenger right away.

Me: You know, you got a lot of fucking nerve being nice to my face and coming up to me, introducing yourself and shaking my hand. I know about you and Matt.

Crisita: What are you talking about?

Me: Do you really think I'm that stupid?

Crisita: I have no idea what you're talking about? Seriously Matt? When I've been all over Josh? Really come on now! I'm friends with all of them but Matt. Really?

Me: You're going to sit there and tell me that you two didn't get a hotel room together 10 days before I went into the hospital?

Crisita: No, I didn't get a hotel with Matt...I hung out with him at the Tiki Bar but me get a hotel room when I live in the Cape...no I'm good thanks...I helped him get to his car yes I did that because the man was drunk out of his mind. But get a room no that wasn't me sorry wrong person.

Me: You're lying.

Crisita: I didn't know about you until I was helping him to his car and he told me about you. But get a room with him no I didn't get a room with him Christina.

Me: You left the key on the nightstand the next morning. You left early cause you had to tutor someone.

Crisita: I had a key yes because he was drunk at the Tiki Bar. He was there I was in the area he messaged me I went hung out he was drunk. I left the key after opening the door and told him to call me in the morning and would help him to his car. He was drunk. I live in the Cape I didn't need to stay in no hotel.

Me: You're still lying. I saw all the messages on Facebook Messenger. You messaged him about not holding you all through the night.

At that point, she knew I had her and Matt caught in a lie. Red handed, and trying to stumble over words wasn't her strong suit.

Crisita: OMG! Please call me Christina because I can't do this over Facebook Messenger. I am not a liar. Please call me. I'm not a yeller either so please don't yell at me. I've been trying to get all of this off my chest. I just didn't want to upset you or cause any problems.

Well that's what I did. I called her. I called her every name in the book too. The one thing I cannot stand are nasty groupies. They are the down fall of so many relationships. The only other thing I despise is a boyfriend that can't keep his dick in his pants. I woke Matt up by smacking him in the face calling him every name in the book as well. He denied it too until after I told him I had talked to her. After all of this, Matt told me he fell in love with me all over again after my surgery and my attitude had changed. He told me he wasn't going to leave me for Crisita. She wasn't too happy about that, so the stalking began. The phone calls started coming in the middle of the night too and the messages started on Facebook. The twitter blasts. It was like I was reliving high school all over again.

***

Matt and I continued to work on things over the next couple of months. I forgave him, but it always haunted me. The visions and nightmares I would get of him and Crisita having sex would put me in a secret depression that I never revealed. I pretended and put on that mask that I was so accustomed to now of appearing to be someone else. It always felt better to be someone else rather than me. The façade of my life was so real to me. Pretending nothing hurt, nothing moved me and no one meant anything to me became such a routine that real life didn't exist in my world. Then one day, out of the blue, Matt asked me if I wanted to get some cocaine. I thought about it for a minute and told him I didn't know if that was a good idea. I explained to him I had a problem with it in my early twenties and remembered what a grave mistake it was. I told him about how my mom detoxed me with copious amounts of black Italian espresso coffee and that I'd been clean for 25 years up until now. Matt was going to get it regardless, but it didn't mean I had to do it. Unfortunately, when you are given an ultimatum, sometimes your heart gets in the way of making the right decisions.

"Well, I'm going to get some. We can have fun and party together or you can be the downer. It's up to you. But if you don't party with me, you can bet I'll find someone who will" he snapped. I knew exactly what that meant. He was going to find another groupie to get high with and cheat on me again.

I certainly didn't want to be a downer and feeling like I already wasn't enough, I would have to be on the same level, or he'd be a downer. I didn't want him to go off and cheat on me again, so I agreed. That was the start of my downward spiral that would last for the next ten months. But that night, sacrificing my 25 years of sobriety for him, I was going to be enough.

CHRISTINA GIORDANO

CHAPTER 6

THE DEMON COMETH

***

Watch out for false prophets. They come to you in sheep's clothing, but inwardly they are ferocious wolves. ~ *Matthew 7:15*

Drugs gave me wings, and then they slowly took away my sky. Addiction is a demon that you wage war on from the inside out. You don't see it happening until it's too late. It's an internal prison that holds you so tight that your world falls apart around you and you don't even notice it. It's the only prison where the shackles are on the inside. What's the harm in snorting a little cocaine on a Friday and Saturday night? All day Sunday there's time to recuperate and fix what you messed up over the weekend; that was Matt's and my view on it. We got high every weekend. We easily went through an eight ball, which is 3.5 grams in a weekend. No big deal. It was fun. We were together and he loved the fact that I'd turned into the perpetual party girl. I was able to control it at first, or so I thought. Friday and Saturday night turned into Thursday, Friday and Saturday night. Then it was Wednesday, Thursday, Friday and Saturday. And so, it continued over the next 3 months. We always left Sunday as our dry out day so we could be responsible adults on Monday morning. Cocaine made us feel like rock stars. Matt and I would get into these deep conversations about life and what we have done in the past. I never revealed too much to him because I suppose inside me somewhere I didn't trust him with such intimate things. But I felt like a superhero. I was enough, or was I? No, I wasn't. I was still competing for Matt's affection, risking my health and self-esteem. This time her name was *Cocaine* and not Crisita.

Even though we were out often in public places high as kites, I always *seemed* to maintain my cool. Matt sometimes had a hard time standing up on his own two feet. He would get totally drunk and then disappear for an hour. He was always scoring blow for us. He would come back into the bar all coked up and flying high. One night, about 2 months into our journey with this white - powdered demon, he fell to the floor in a one of our favorite local bars revealing a bag of cocaine in his hand. I had to wrestle it out of his hand, get him up off the floor because well, the dude was making a scene. Holding a gram of cocaine wrapped up in your hand and your drunken ass on the ground isn't very subtle. A friend of mine helped me get him home to put him in bed, but the drugs came back to the bar with me, to enjoy the local original bands and the company of my friends.

***

I never saw what was coming when Andy walked in while we were all hanging out together. Andy was a well-known guitarist for a local band called, *Before the Fire*. We were friends and he was always kind to me. In fact, all the members of *Before the Fire* were friends of mine. I never thought of

Andy as sexy, nor did I have any attraction to him. He was tall and lanky with long brown hair and blue eyes. He had tattoo sleeves on both of his forearms that covered part of his hands. Later I would find out that there was a reason for this many tattoos; he was hiding track marks. He was also an egotistical little ass and everyone knew he was a junkie. Andy loved his drugs and people loved him for it. I always wanted to get to know him better just because of the music. I was standing on the side of the stage when Andy walked up to me. He hugged me and greeted me like he always did, nice and sweet like. He then turned and walked away while I continued to listen to the band. I found myself looking back at him, almost uncontrollably. He was obviously looking at me too and shot me the greatest smile. I finally got the courage to say something to him.

I shouted, "Hey, come here!" It was loud in there with all that hard rock music saturating the air that night. He smiled and walked over to me and when he leaned his ear close to my lips, I could smell his cologne. I really liked it and him all of a sudden!

"You want to go out to my car and do a bump?" I asked devilishly.

"Well, hell yeah!" he said with the happiest look on his face and his raised eyebrows like he was shocked I wanted to get high with him. My high made him look extra hot that night for some reason. Even though I had never had any attraction to him before, that night was different. So off to my car we went. As I took the baggie out of my wallet, I realized how high I was as my hands were shaking. Or was it Andy that had that effect on me, who knows. I cut a line with my bankcard and took the first hit. I never trusted anyone to do the first line. I was taught this twenty-five years ago when I had my first go around with cocaine. People who do the first line of *your* drugs will snort half of the second line as well, leaving you with nothing but a small bit. Even though Matt paid for it, it was mine now because he was passed out at home. After I finished my line I passed the cocaine over to Andy. I was always fair and generous. I always made sure the lines were even for people I shared it with because it's just not good drugging ethic to invite someone to the party and then short them. Just writing that makes me feel amazed that I even had manners when it came to drugs, like it was really important. The cocaine hit my nose and head very quickly. It was good product, even Andy commented on that as well.

"Good god woman! Where did you get that shit? That stuff is on fire!"

"I don't know where Matt got it. He's at home passed out and I'm here with you. That's all that matters. Want to do another one?"

"Hell yeah, I do", Andy said with abnormal passion. When he said, 'Hell yeah, I do.", that meant he meant business!

So, we did another line and the night for Andy and I went on just like that; go into the bar and enjoy the band for a bit and then disappear into my car for another fix. At some point, my opinion of Andy changed. He started talking to me about life, and me.

"You know Christina, I always liked you", he said looking right into my eyes.

"Thanks Andy, I always liked you too. We've had our differences in our philosophies of music but all in all, I think your pretty cool. And right now, I'm enjoying partying with you." I said that with vulnerability he couldn't miss or hopefully resist. We did another line, headed back to the bar and just before we got to the door, Matt walked up to us, all sobered up and agitated.

"Where are my drugs?" No hello or thanks for carrying my sorry ass home, just where are my drugs? I looked at Andy and then Matt and said, "What drugs?"

"The drugs I bought earlier! You know exactly what I mean. Now hand them over."

"Matt, I have no idea what you're talking about! All I did was take you home earlier because they were kicking you out for passing out on the floor and making a scene!"

"I fell on the floor? Fuck! I must have dropped the baggie when I did. Damn. Oh well, I'll get more later," Matt said as he finally noticed Andy standing right next to me, "Hey Andy, what's happening man, come in with me and Christina and let me buy you a drink."

***

Andy was never one to say no to a freebee so the three of us trotted into the bar and ordered our drinks. Matt liked to pay for shit when other people were around. I suppose it made him feel like a man. But when it was just me and him he was cheapest guy you ever net. Matt wound up getting more cocaine and Andy came with us to my apartment because at the time, he had nowhere to sleep. His ride was leaving and asked if I would give him a ride home. I couldn't say no because I found a new fondness for Andy and enjoyed hanging out with him. But when the clock struck four o'clock a.m., I couldn't drive but the 2 minutes down the road to my apartment. When we go to my place, the first thing I did was go change my clothes. This was going to be a long night so I wanted to get into something a bit more comfortable. I was so high it was ridiculous. I have the most awesome back porch for parties. I have a hot tub that is in the ground, a couch and a nice sitting area where people can gather and hang out. Andy hadn't been to my house before so he was thoroughly impressed how I lived. This made me feel good someone liked and appreciated what I have, unlike Matt who always took it all for granted. He'd stay with me for months and never contribute a dime to the house rent or bills. In retrospect how rude was that and how dumb was I to let that happen? He had enough for drugs, but not enough to help out with bills. We all got into the hot tub and had a heavy drug-induced philosophical babbling conversation that meant nothing as we continued to do more blow. This went on until seven o'clock in the morning. The drugs finally ran out so Matt went to sleep. It was just Andy and I sitting out on the back porch. I reached into my pocket and pulled out a baggie I had snatched from Matt while he wasn't looking. Andy and I continued to party until it was time for us to stop. There comes a point when partying like this doesn't make sense. There just isn't any more of the high left, unless one wants to overdose. He asked if I would take him home and I reluctantly did so considering how totally messed up I was.

***

We didn't hear from Andy for about four weeks after that night. Matt and I had an argument about my cats meowing and keeping him up at night so I suggested he go back and live with his Dad. He was never fond of Natasha and Ace. He used to throw nerf like baseballs at them to keep them away from him. Instead of going back to his Dad's, which I found out later that he was kicked out of his Dad's house, he had rented a nice house with a friend of his and decided he needed his space, so he said. That lasted all of a few days as he learned that I had hooked up with his dealer, Rick. I had to start dealing cocaine to afford my own habit. I was making money and getting high. What could be better than that! Matt glued himself to me now more than ever because I had the drugs now. I was in control and it felt good. I dealt to a lot of the locals at our favorite bar, including some of the employees. When I walked through the door, everyone's eyes would light up because *I* had the drugs. *I* was needed and important now. It was like I finally reached the *celebrity* status *I* wanted and needed. *I* was finally in control of people and *I* had what they wanted. I was known as the *'Snow Queen'*. How fucked up is it that I'm a Disney character who deals coke! My clients would input my phone number as *'Elsa'* from the movie *'Frozen'*; considering it is one of my favorite Disney movies. So, if you ever go through someone's phone down here in Cape Coral, Florida and you see a contact name as 'Elsa', you'll know I was his or her supplier. As was routine, I would go to the dealer about three times a week and get my stash which usually consisted of about seven grams, known as a 'Vick". The name "Vick" come from Michael Vicks jersey number being "7". Matt was doing so much cocaine he couldn't keep up with me financially. He suddenly owed me a lot of money, something that's easy to do when one has a cocaine habit like Matt's. He would pawn his guitars mid-week and get them out right before his gigs on Friday nights after he got paid. It's like stealing from Peter to pay Paul. It's a vicious cycle that eventually catches up to you and before you know it, you either don't have the money to pay the pawn man or you don't have the money to pay for your drugs or worse, your dead. Either way, it's a lose-lose situation. But the best part for me was my drugs were for the most part free. Then one night, while Matt and I were on our way to his gig, Andy called in a panic.

"Christina, please come and get me. I'm not in a good place. I need help," Andy sounded so desperate on the phone that my heart broke for him because I found out that he was a 'booter'. A 'booter' is someone who shoots drugs with a needle into their veins. It can be any drug like cocaine, heroin, oxycodone, and dilauded. Just about any drug can be taken intravenously. Even crack can be liquidized with white distilled vinegar and pulled into a needle and shot up. It's the purest form of cocaine and can send you flying into outer space. Trust me, I did it quite a lot of it. I told Matt I need to help Andy but Matt was worried about me going down there to get Andy by myself. We had no idea what kind of people Andy was shacked up with in downtown Fort Myers. Matt said no and grabbed the phone from me. I was dumbfounded that he cared so much about me, in fact, this may have been the first time I had ever seen him actually show he cared. But then again, I'd be worried too if something might happen to my drug supplier in uncharted territory. I mean shit! The night would suck if my drug supplier went down. But, Matt let me go anyway. Thinking about this now, why didn't he come with me?

When I arrived at the "Sea Chest Inn" in downtown Fort Myers, Florida, Andy was out in the parking lot waiting for me. He invited me in. I almost didn't want to but I was curious and as I walked through the door it looked like the typical crack house, dark and depressing and worse than I ever imagined it to be. There were people laying all over the place. Needles and tourniquets on the table. People snorting, shooting and smoking drugs. The room smelled rank and actually gave me an uneasy feeling. Then the phone rang. It was Matt.

"Babe, are you ok?"

"Yeah I'm fine. I'm here with Andy, getting a few things and we'll be over to the gig shortly."

"Ok. I'm just checking up on you. Let me talk to Andy", Matt said firmly and I told him to hang on and handed the phone over to Andy.

"What's up bro?" Andy said calmly. I could hear Matt talking on the other line.

"Andy, don't you let anything happen to her, you understand? If anything happens to her, I'll never forgive you. That's my girl. I am putting her life in your hands." Awe, that was nice. Matt cared about me.

"Don't worry brother. Nothing is going to happen to her. I would take a bullet for her."

What? Did I just hear what he said right? Andy would take a bullet for me? Did he really care about me that much? Oh my God! This made me feel like I've never felt before. I'm a real girl who meant something real to someone. I hadn't seen Andy in four weeks but felt like I wanted to get physically closer to him and when I did he put his arm around me as he finished his conversation with Matt. The dealer that had the crack house, named Kasper, walked us out to my car. That was his dealers name and I thought that was a great name for a cocaine dealer. He asked me if I needed a bag of cocaine. Duh! Of course I did, so I said yes but I wanted to want to try it first. He shook my hand slipping a gram of cocaine in a baggie onto my hand. That was a huge gesture as a gram of cocaine goes for about sixty dollars to eighty dollars around here depending if its booting quality or bar quality. I thanked him and told him I would get back to him. The moment Andy and I got in my car, I had to try a bump and holy cow that shit was good! I gave some to Andy and there we were again, on our way for another night of partying like the rock stars we thought we were! Since I rescued Andy that night, he considered Matt and me his family. We were like a sister and brother to him, but what he really was, was a hardcore drug addict, nothing like Matt and I ever imagined. From that night on, Andy spent every weekend with us, either at Matt's house or my apartment. The three of us were inseparable. I would walk into the bar and people's eyes were always fixed on the three of us. It was like I had two boyfriends or bodyguards. I was the envy of every person. People wanted my drugs and wanted to be me. One night this girl came up to me and in a real snotty voice she said, "Hey, come here." Was she really talking to me like that?

"Yes? Can I help you?" I said sarcastically.

"Yeah, you can. Who's your source?"

"My what?" I said completely taken back.

"I said, *who is your source?*" Her arrogant attitude made me angry so I answered her in the same arrogant tone but only with much more conviction.

"Oh honey, *I am the source.*" I said firmly and without much facial expression.

"You're the source?" She sounded puzzled.

Bored with the conversation, I rolled my eyes, shook my head at her and walked away. Yes, as popular as I was and as loved for drugs as I was, there were people that had no clue as to how I supplemented my income or supported my habit. But she wanted something that I had and far be it for me to say no to a sale. It ended up being such a busy night. I sold 26 grams of cocaine that night. I needed to ante up *four* times that night with the dealer. I had a shitload of cash left over for my rent and my car payment and even some fun money for me! I was killing it. And I had Andy following me around like a Pit bull protecting me from everyone and consequently making sales for me, which he would get rewarded for. Every time he made a sale for me, I would give him a line. This particular night though was the beginning of my spiraling downward into the abyss, which lasted for the next 5 months. Also, Andy and I were growing closer and closer while Matt and I started fading away.

***

After the gig that night, we all hobbled off to my place for the traditional Friday night after party. I went and changed like I always did when we got home. When I came out of my bedroom Matt was standing in the kitchen looking very disturbed.

"Christina, don't move. Stay over there", he said gesturing his hand over to the bedroom, "you don't need to see this."

"What! What is it? Is Andy ok?" I got worried as Matt was looking at the floor by the stove although I couldn't see all the way into the kitchen because the island was blocking what Matt was looking at. Far be it for me to listen to anyone anymore, so I walked around the kitchen island. I was worried that something happened to Andy as I heard him grunting in the kitchen. Matt tried to cut me off but it was too late and then I saw it. I saw Andy kneeling on the floor on one knee with a tourniquet on his left forearm with a needle sticking out of the back of his hand. I got there just as he pushed the plunger down on himself. He took the tourniquet off and then pulled the needle out of the back of his hand and licked his puncture mark. I was stunned. No words. Then, Andy looked up at me with shame, like I would disapprove of him for doing something like this. But I didn't disapprove of him, I felt sorry for him. And yet at the same time, he had the most peaceful look on his face and I wanted that peace. We locked eyes as Matt was holding me back. In that instant, believe it or not, Andy looked unbelievably sexy to me. The way I saw it, the whole idea of slamming a needle in your body with drugs in it took courage, and was incredibly masculine and sexy to me. What a warped mindset I had and what was I setting myself up for? A man shooting drugs into his veins was sexy to me? Really? And as soon as the thrashing high hit Andy's head, he nodded his gorgeous and peaceful face at me and licked his lips. Oh man, his lips were so beautiful I could've kissed him right there and then. Most people would think that it would be a sickening sight, but to me it was heavenly. Everyone knew Andy did that with his drugs, but to actually see it done was something I will never forget. An insatiable feeling came over me and as Matt let me go I raced across the kitchen to hug Andy. He wrapped his arms around me tight without hesitating. This guy had charisma and I wanted it.

"I'm sorry Christina, I didn't want you to see that and think bad things of me."

"I could never think bad things about you. We all do drugs here. Doesn't matter how we do them. We all do them," I said trying to ease his conscience and mine. "I would rather you feel comfortable doing it front of me than to have to hide it. You consider me your family, right?" I asked as he nodded his head yes. "Then family needs to trust each other."

I look back on it now, and I'm not quite sure if I would be able to handle seeing that now. I'd more than likely be repulsed by it. Yeah, that would be a definite, big fat no for me to ever be around that shit again! But back then it was the peace I saw in his eyes, not the addiction. In my mind, he found undeniable peace, or so it seemed. After that night, my heart went out to Andy even more. He always told me that the high of shooting up was totally different than the high you got from snorting it. He would let me watch him shoot up in the bathroom. He even let me help him by holding the tourniquet for him. It was a bond that we shared together. It was an intimacy I shared with no one else. He trusted me enough to assist him and me being a part of his world. Not that I was in love with him but as he was my family and well, we were all addicts, we just chose different methods to administer our high and that was ok with me. I was so messed up back then so everything was okay for me. As long as I could keep Andy, Matt and the drugs around, life was perfect, at least for a little while.

***

I had a suspicion that Matt was cheating on me again so I distanced myself from him. Besides, Andy was stuck to me like glue, partying together and having a grand old time. Andy always made me feel good about myself. When we were headed out on the town, I would come out of my bedroom dressed up, my hair perfect and my make up on point and he would always compliment me on how sexy or pretty I looked. Matt never complimented me. I tried so hard to look pretty for Matt but he never noticed. I suppose he was too busy contemplating on which groupie he was going to sneak off and cheat on me with while I wasn't paying attention. When Andy and I would go out, Andy was always focused on me. I was enough for Andy. We had the best friendship, at least in my eyes at the time. He always called me his best friend and he would say it with every conviction in his heart, or so it seemed. He trusted me with some very intimate secrets about his life and family. Were they true? I don't know about all that now, but back then it seemed like it was true. Drugs do that to you. Then slowly but surely, it turned into more than that. We were on our way out one night and while we were getting ready, Andy and I were having a conversation about our friendship. It was a Friday night and we were both sober while getting ready so this was a rare occasion when we opened up to each other.

"You know, I was talking to one of the guys at work today. He asked me if you were my girlfriend and I told him no, but she's an amazing woman and she's my best friend. She took me in when I had nowhere to go and she actually put clothes on my back and made sure I ate. I owe a lot to you Christina. I would walk through fire for you and take a bullet to protect you. I hope you know that." Boy, did he sound convincing that night.

"I know that Andy. I would do the same for you. I know we are just roomies, but you have been more of a hero to me than Matt has ever tried to be. I just want you to be happy and I want you to enjoy your life." I said all of this while laying out two lines of cocaine on the glass top of my dresser. The sober conversation didn't last long.

"Is one of those for me I hope?" He asked.

"Of course! When have I denied you anything since you've entered my life?" I responded in a tone that was foreign to me.

"Never."

As Andy walked over to do the line, he locked eyes with me. My heart started beating like it was going to fly out of my chest. Just when I thought he was finally going to kiss me, he grabbed the straw from me and leaned over to snort the cocaine. He handed me the straw and gave me a look I could swear had a sexual overtone to it. I took the straw out of his hand slowly with a sort of caress to it as he held onto my hand never looking away from my eyes. I smiled back at him and giggled while shaking my head. I snorted my line and packed our paraphernalia up for a big night of sales, but as I followed him out of the bedroom I grabbed his arm.

"Andy, with you living here with me, it's inevitable that something will eventually happen. We get to fucked up and have too many deep conversations while we're fucked up for it not to happen. We are both basically alone. You have no one and even though Matt is somewhat in the picture, he doesn't want me for anything but the drugs."

"Christina, I know it will happen and when it does, it does. It will happen when it's supposed to. But I'm telling you now, I don't like the way Matt treats you. He uses you for the drug supply. He's never around until when he needs a bag and that makes me mad. You will always come first with me, friendship or otherwise. I love you."

"I love you too Andy", I said as he was closing in on my space again.

Then it happened. He kissed me as passionately as I've wanted to be kissed for the last two and a half years I'd been with Matt. My face flushed, my body trembled. He put his hand up to my face, holding it gently in his hand as he reached behind my head, slightly grabbing a handful of my hair while tilting my head back to control where he wanted me to be. His lips were warm, wet and fascinating. I was high on cocaine but Andy got me higher as his tongue explored my mouth while holding me around my waist. I was his, he owned me. For that moment, I was his and he was mine. Even though we were never in a relationship per say, but for that brief instant, my heart belonged to him. He broke away from my lips, kissing them again quickly. He explored my eyes, trying to read what I was thinking as if he was looking straight at the mirrors of my soul.

"Well, how was that?" he asked staring at me with those beautiful blue eyes.

"Amazing, absolutely amazing", I said back with a whisper in my voice.

"Matt will never kiss you like that. And if I have anything to do with it, he will never kiss you again. You deserve better than him. Are you ready to go out now?"

Feeling as though I was floating, I nodded yes and out the door we went. I locked the front door and as I turned around, there he was standing nose to nose with me. He took the keys out of my hand and gave me a quick kiss on the lips.

"I'm the man in this relationship, friendship, or whatever you want to call what we have going on. When you go out with me, you're the lady; you will not drive unless I am too fucked up to drive, got it? You aren't a chauffeur; you are a woman and you will be treated like one." He said that with such an authoritative tone that I had no choice but to let him. When we arrived at Matt's gig, it was a night I will never forget. Andy stayed stuck to me all night long. He even slow danced with me to *'Purple Rain'* by Prince, the Artist. I sold Matt a lot of cocaine that night and it was funny to watch Andy work Matt over saying I wouldn't give him any so Matt would give up most of his shit to Andy and I would sell Matt another bag. Matt kept looking at how close Andy and I were that night. I think he had a feeling that something was going on. I suppose Matt got a little heated about that since I was supposed to be his girlfriend, but only when it was convenient for him. As far as I was concerned, it wasn't convenient for Matt to be my boyfriend.

CHAPTER 7

THE DEMON TAKETH AWAY

***

His tail swept down a third of the stars of heaven and cast them to the earth. And the dragon stood before the woman who was about to give birth, so that when she bore her child he might devour it. ~ Revelation 12:4

I used to have flashbacks, trying to picture how Matt and Crisita would look while having sex together and afterwards. It burned my brain something fierce, especially when I was high. Subsequently, I would just get higher. I could never get high enough to get those images out of my head. I couldn't ever get high enough to find peace. I wanted Matt to have images of me having sex with another man but then when I thought about it later, I knew it really wasn't the answer. But at the time, it gave me a fantastic idea. I continued to make myself non-accessible to Matt and more accessible to Andy. I would go to work and be an adult all day and then rush home right after to be with Andy because I couldn't wait to hang out with him. It was like he had this control over my heart, my mind and body. I couldn't think for myself anymore. It was like he entered my brain and did all my thinking for me. I believe now that it was undoubtedly called a mind-fuck or better yet, infinite manipulation. But to me, it was Andy caring about how I felt and he always made sure I felt like I was important. It's what eventually keeps us girls around. I mean you can't tell me that no woman wants to feel important to someone. I felt needed by everyone and I was enough for Andy. Or so he made me believe.

***

Andy and I went to the pick-up point to score my stash from Rick, the drug dealer, as we headed out to another one of Matts gigs. Andy got used to shooting cocaine while in front of me so when we would leave the pick-up point, I would immediately pour some into a bottle cap for him so he could mix his concoction on the little piece of cotton with water to draw up into his rig while I was driving. A 'rig' is what us drug addicts call the needle. It didn't faze me anymore to watch Andy get high, but it sure started making me curious. The more I watched him shoot up, the more I wanted to feel the peace that he felt. I deserved to feel that peace. I couldn't remember the last time I felt peaceful at all. They say peace comes from within. I saw it as an administration of drugs. To find peace is to be better equipped to face the world. Sometimes that becomes your inner battle and the battle is self-control. The battle is to take it captive. I mean, if we let ourselves get out of control, there is no peace. The difference is with addicts, we think we are in control when in reality, our substance of choice controls us. This is not the life we want, but the life we need at the time of active addiction to control the suppression and numb our pain. Which then results in an uncontrollable pain that is much worse once the numbness wears off. I wanted to be numb all the time. My quest for peace came at a very high price. But I continued to just watch and every time he did it, he continued to get more and more sexy to me. Andy was becoming my peace.

Matt started becoming a real pain in the ass lately and I really didn't feel like going to his gig, but Andy liked sitting in with Matt's band and playing guitar and I enjoyed singing a few songs with the band as well. Andy and I loved to laugh and make fun at the lead singer's girlfriend, Kat. She always tried to score a line or a bump of cocaine off of all my clients while her boyfriend, was totally clueless to what was going on with her. In fact, recently, even after her calling me a junkie and a coke head, during the reunion show for Andy's band in November of 2016, she tried scoring some cocaine by following a few of my close friends around the local bar. Andy always called her a freak and a coke whore but I guess when you're that desperate, you'll do anything. Until this day, that poor lead singer has no idea who he is dating. But Kat wasn't my focus that night, Andy was. I noticed Matt kept eyeing this woman at the bar who looked older than me so I took this opportunity into my own hands. I told Matt that Andy and I were going over to the local R Bar to make a drop and we would be back later. I figured I'd ditch Matt before he had a chance to ditch me. So, Andy and I headed over to our local hot spot and continued to drink and enjoy the local music as always and continued to get high, obviously. A girl that Andy had been hanging around with when I was with Matt which was now a rare occasion was there and she was with another guy making it very obvious, trying to get Andy's blood boiling. Andy came over and told me all about her. I didn't like when people hurt Andy and he didn't like when people hurt me.

"She's here with some dude and making an ass out of herself," Andy said with a shrug.

"So, what are you going to do?" I said hoping that he would leave with me that night.

"I'm going to kiss you right here and right now because I'm with you tonight and she means nothing to me."

Before I could get another word in, Andy kissed me in public. We were standing right in the middle of the bar in front of the stage. I was totally stunned by what he did.

"Are you sure that was a smart thing to do?" I asked.

"Yes, it was the perfect thing to do."

Damn, he was a smooth operator. That's for sure! Andy knew I was a little upset about Matt eyeing that old lady at the previous bar, so he was trying to comfort me by putting me on that priority pedestal that Matt always put himself on. When in reality, he was trying to make sure his 'Snow Queen' serviced his drug needs. I can't lie; it made me feel good when he treated me like that. He always said the right things and considering I was always fucked up, I believed every word of it. You see when you suffer great pain and the feeling that you aren't enough and then all of a sudden someone you thought was untouchable, shows you that kind of attention and is half way decent looking, you soak it up. It's all you want. You crave being enough for someone; and with Andy I was more than enough. He made me believe his sun set and his moon rose with me in it.

***

That night we never went back to pick up Matt. We went home and did all the drugs ourselves, just him and me. When the drugs ran out I went to my room and Andy settled into the couch, which had become his bed. I tossed and turned for a few minutes that felt like hours. Finally, I got up and stood at my bedroom door.

"Andy, are you asleep yet?"

"No way, I'm too high to fall asleep right now."

"Andy, can you sleep with me tonight? I need you to hold me."

"Of course, sweetheart. I thought you'd never ask."

Andy got off the couch, walked over to me and I wrapped my arms around him.

"Come on sweetheart, let's get you into bed."

"Ok, but I sleep naked so, watch your hands!"

Andy chuckled and led me to the bed with his hand on my lower back. We climbed into bed in the dark and I proceeded to take my clothes off.

Natasha, my Russian Siberian cat jumped on the bed with us and lay between us. She's a very snuggly affectionate cat and loved Andy, which is always a good sign in my book. Andy was always kind to my pets. Not like Matt. Andy was always feeding them treats and petting them. He would even walk my little girl Chihuahuas when I was at work. Natasha has this very strong, very hard purr. In Russia, they are considered wild cats, not feral, but wild. She always helped me go to sleep when I was high. It's like she knew something was wrong. She always knows when something isn't right with me, so her purring was very soothing for us.

Immediately after getting into bed, Andy faced me, kissing and licking my lips. I followed his lead and kissed him back. He made my body tremble like no one else. I'm sure the amount of cocaine I did that night had something to do with me shaking, but my heart was pounding in my ears as he grabbed a hold of my waist and brought my naked body closer to his, wrapping his arms around me. His hand caressed the small of my back, feeling every inch of my back until he got to the base of my neck. He grabbed my hair like he did the first night he kissed me. All the while he continued to plunge his tongue inside my mouth like a hungry animal that hadn't eaten in days. His breathing got heavier and I could hear myself moan in his mouth. I wanted all of him. I wanted everything from Andy. I wanted to share everything with him. I wanted to be his. Natasha jumped off the bed as she knew something was about to happen. He suddenly rolled me over in the spoon position, grabbed my waist tightly with one hand and firmly grasped my hair with the other. And then it happened. He entered me forcefully as I accepted him totally with my heart, my soul and my body. With as much force as he made love to me, he was gently kissing my neck and my shoulder while breathing and whispering in my ear.

"You are my home Christina. You're my home. You are mine." Andy said with a heated breath in my ear while tasting my neck with his mouth

"Only for you, Andy. Only for you." I said like a woman madly in love.

"And no one else." He made that statement adamantly with a hard pull of my hair, with a biting kiss on my neck that sent my world spinning and chills down my spine. I let out a soft wild cry as my orgasm hit me like a cascading waterfall as Andy climaxed at the same time. In my heart, we were each other's. In my mind, we were the greatest drug-dealing team of all time. We had it all. We were best friends, we loved each other like brother and sister, and in some insatiable, incestuous rationale, we were lovers; plus we were awesome at doing drugs together. I will always remember the first time I had sex with Andy. It took away my need for Matt. But I still wanted more. I wanted to be on Andy's level. I still needed my peace and I still needed to show Matt that I didn't need him. Like some sick Sid Vicious and Nancy Spungen movie remake, it was now Andy and I.

I remember falling asleep that night in Andy's arms thinking of nothing but the peace I needed to feel. I just needed my peace and I somehow got it for a brief minute through that escape with him in my bed. I look back on it now and that was just the start of the deceit and the lying. The very things that brought life to a screeching halt. It went on for months. I wanted nothing more than to throw that into Matt's face and finally say, "Look! You aren't the only one that people desire. You aren't the only one that people want to have sex with. Look at me! I'm enough for someone!" Matt never loved me the way I wanted him to. He was too much in love with himself and too much in love with the idea of others wanting him and cheating on me time and time again.

***

Matt had gigs every weekend and more and more Andy and I would go for a little bit and then escape to go make a run or a deal. We were moving a lot of cocaine but we were also doing a lot. He would disappear outside to shoot up in my car while I would go to the bathroom and do my lines. One night, he decided to just snort cocaine with me and man did we have fun. That was the first night Andy was worried about losing me. We were once again headed out to Matts gig. We made a detour first to a bar in downtown Fort Myers known to everyone as the 'Cigar Bar.' It was the hot place in town and still is to this day one of my favorites, although I don't go in there much anymore because it's a huge trigger for me from the past. We were going to meet a friend of ours down there and consequently later found out that he had come and gone. When we got out of the car after snorting two big fat lines, we headed down to the bar. As we walked, Andy looked over at me and I said, "Andy, I do believe you are looking quite sexy tonight". His comment back was all I needed to hear to put me on cloud nine. I walked beside him elated to be with him that evening because his response was amazing. "Well, Miss Giordano, I do believe you are looking quite sexy yourself and I'm thoroughly proud to be walking beside you this evening as well." Like I said, he was a real smooth talker but to actually get a compliment that I didn't have to ask for is what made me feel like a million bucks that night, and as the evening went on I just kept feeling better and better. We finally made it to Matt's gig back at this seedy little bar in Cape Coral's entertainment district. Matt had been texting me the whole time Andy and I were gallivanting around town and when we walked in the bar we looked like the couple of the year. Both of us were dressed up and Andy's hair was down because he never wore it in a ponytail when we went out. He knew I liked it down and he wanted his drugs for free so he would always try to please me. Matt's eyes showed me how disturbed he was when we walked in. After the last song of the bands set, Matt walked up to us.

"So, where were you two?"

"We went downtown first to meet Mike." I retorted with the same attitude that he gave me.

"Oh yeah? How was downtown then?" Oh boy he was pissed off but I tried to remain cool about it.

"It was great Matt, thanks for asking. Andy actually gave me a compliment too. So where's my forty bucks?" I figured I would get right to the point of why he wanted me there earlier.

"You re-up'd? Cool. Here's eighty bucks," he handed me four twenty dollar bills, "Give me two bags." In case you're wondering what re-up'd means; it's when the dealer gives you a fresh supply of drugs.

I handed Matt the bags. He kissed me on the lips before he walked away. I wiped my mouth of his spit and looked over at Andy. His lips were straight as an arrow and his nostrils were flared. Clearly, he was pissed at Matt for kissing me. After all, when the boyfriend of your drug supplier is kissing her, there's a good possibility that she might end up going home with him that night and then the drug supply is gone. In this case, this wasn't going to happen. Not a chance.

***

Andy stayed close to me to me the rest of the night, never letting me out of his sight, not even when Kat came around and started tapping the side of her nose at us wanting more free drugs. She really got on my nerves. I got smart after a while and always kept a bag around that was mostly Tylenol crushed up for her to snort because it would get her off my tail for a while. And per usual, she would go do her random hounding of my customers and eventually they would tell her to get lost as well. Andy always followed me out to the car when making a deal or when little miss coke fiend was getting antsy. He wanted to make sure nothing happened to me. He called himself my protector when in reality; he was only there to protect his supply.

Towards the end of the night, we were invited back for an after party. Matt wasn't invited and so it was just Andy and me, *His Sid to my Nancy*. We escaped under the radar of Matt and drove across town. The couple that we were hanging out with that night was always very nice to me and accepted Andy over to their house as trusted by me. As the conversation and sexual innuendos went on into the morning hours, Andy and I kept doing line after line and the couple kept drinking and drinking while Matt kept calling and texting. I wasn't going to answer him, no way. I was with my Andy and nothing could take me away from him. He made me feel so pretty, sexy and wanted. I was always enough for him. Drugs can make you think anything you want. In reality, nothing is a reality when your high or strung out. At some point in my totally obliterated mind, I started making out with the wife. Matt always wanted a threesome and said that if I had a threesome then he wouldn't have to always cheat on me. I suppose I wanted to see what Andy's reaction would be while he watched me make out with another woman. He watched as the drunken husband kept talking to Andy and as I looked up while still kissing the wife I saw Andy's eyes. His expression was priceless. He didn't know what to think and I'm supposed to be the woman he cared about. Here I was kissing another woman and I kind of enjoyed it, but I'm not sure what Andy thought about it. The couple eventually went to bed while Andy and I did one more lines. When I lifted my head back up from the plate I was snorting on, he grabbed a fist full of my hair, (he liked doing that I guess), and looked me straight in the eye as he maneuvered me up against the kitchen counter. Tilting my head back by the hair that was entangled in his fist so I could look straight back at him he said, "You know I love you right?"

"Yes." I said with a gazed out and totally stunned look. Andy tilted my head, exposing my neck. He began kissing and lightly biting my neck with his teeth. He finally thrust his tongue into my mouth wildly, like he owned me while whispering in my ear. I thought he either hated or loved the fact that I kissed another woman.

"You're mine tonight Christina. Only mine." Well I guess that answers that thought. He didn't like it.

"Yes. Okay, I'm sorry." I whispered back trying to catch my breath as Andy sent chills down my spine like he does each and every time he wants me. That feeling always goes down my legs and comes back up my jugular. Right then, in the quiet dark of the room, my phone rang. It was Matt. I figured I better answer it as I had already avoided multiple calls from him throughout the night for too long.

"Hey, where are you?"

"I'm at an after party with Andy."

"Come and get me. I'm at an after party at Bob's place and these people are driving me nuts."

"Hold on", I put my hand over the phone and said to Andy, "Matt wants us to go pick him up."

"Christina, the only reason why Matt wants you to go and get him is because he's out of coke."

"Andy, I can't leave him there." My God, I had empathy even when I was strung out. That's really dangerous. I got back on the phone with Matt.

"Ok, text me the address and we're leaving now".

I hung up the phone with Matt and saw a tear in Andy's eye. He grabbed my arms and wrapped me in a hold I will never forget.

"When we pick up Matt, please don't ignore me. We are starting something here and I don't think I can handle you ignoring me. I wanted it to be just you and me tonight."

I pulled back and looked into his eyes, "I promise I won't ignore you.

You've made my night so special and I'm not going to be with Matt tonight. I'm with you, I promise"

So, with that, we left the couple sleeping in their house and we headed out to go rescue Matt.

Matt was standing outside when we pulled up after driving around aimlessly trying to figure out what crack house he was in. As Matt walked up to the car I told Andy to stay in the front seat. Matt got in the back and he looked like hell had hit him with a two by four. Andy and I looked at each other and all I remember thinking was, 'Geez I need another line'. Time moves fast when you're fucked up. You lose track of the days and you can't remember what you did the night before. But those few days stayed with me. As I write, I remember very vividly what my brain at the time suppressed. Sometimes when I remember certain things I get feverish and it feels like my whole body is on fire. My skin starts to feel like it's crawling. When I think of Andy touching me there is sometimes a peace that takes over and I feel at ease. It takes a long time to recover from a mind-fuck. When you thought someone cared about you and then you start to realize that they didn't truly care, whether they are a friend or someone you love and have a bond with, it's devastating and there's nothing to fill the void. The ultimate *fuck you*.

***

Andy made feel alive, but if I'm going to honest, how do I know how Andy made me feel? I was high all the time! It was the drugs that made me feel alive, but then again even though he had an agenda, I felt what it was like to be cared for and loved, even if it was all make believe and no matter how much of an addict he is. He was a fake. The whole thing was fake. I know that now, but he still made me feel like I was enough. Was I in love with him? No. Was I in love with the façade of being enough for someone even though we were just friends? Yes. For the first time, that night, I felt like I was enough. Even if it was all make believe, it made me feel good. When we returned to Matts house, I had all intentions of dropping him off. This guy Bob had tagged along for the ride and he was just as messed up as Matt was. I had never met this guy before and boy was he a strange character. He brought along a guitar that he had no idea how to play so I ultimately had to tell him to shut up at one point. The three guys hung out in the kitchen while I went quietly to the bathroom to take care of my fix. I laid out the biggest rail of coke and snorted my brains out! I looked in the mirror after putting my stash in my pants to make sure there was no residue and the drip hit the back of my throat instantly. I never felt a drip like that. It felt like liquid metal dripping down the back of my throat. I walked out of the bathroom and rubbed my nose as it felt like it was running and then all of a sudden, my hands were covered in blood. I could taste the blood running into my lips from nose and it just kept running. I walked around the corner to the kitchen and stood away from the guys looking at my hands and said, "Andy? I think something's wrong".

Andy turned to me while he talked to Matt, stopping in mid-sentence as I looked up from my bloody hands. His mouth dropped open as he started walking quickly towards me. Matt was on his tail.

"Sweetheart, what's wrong?"

"Andy, take me home. I want to go home." I was looking blankly into Andy's eyes with my nose pouring out blood as Matt was trying to talk to me.

"Come on baby." Andy said turning to Matt, "I'm taking her home. She's had it for the night. She needs rest. She needs to go to sleep she's been up for three days." We had been up since Thursday. It was now Saturday morning and we had more partying to do later on that night. Matt was trying to keep me there by wiping my nose and my blood-stained hands but Andy wasn't having any of it. Andy put his hand up in front of Matt's face to shut him up as he grabbed my hand and led me outside to the car. When we got home, Andy took two Xanax of mine and crushed them both, chopping them up into two lines and handed me a straw.

"Snort that."

"What?" I said being very puzzled.

"Sort that line."

"It's Xanax! Can you snort Xanax after snorting a copious amount of cocaine?"

"Yes. Do it!" he said very firmly as I jumped. I never heard Andy raise his voice to me like that before.

I did what he said and snorted the line of Xanax as Andy caught the blood coming out of my nose with a piece of toilet paper he had grabbed from the bathroom. I suppose he expected my nose to bleed again. He put me to bed like a doll. Very gently and very caring. He snorted his line, took his clothes off and climbed into bed with me. It was warm and it was comfortable as he wrapped his arms around me while the deep sleep of the Xanax took over. I had my peace. For once in my life I felt peace flow over me as the world around became pitch black.

CHAPTER 8

THE QUICKENING

***

Be sober minded; be watchful. Your adversary the devil prowls around like a roaring lion, seeking someone to devour. ~ 1 Peter 5:8

Every mistake I've made was very well thought out. I'm the type of person who plans things ahead of time. Every major event that's ever happened to me I've planned, and it always went like clockwork. I suppose that's why Karma had a field day with me. She was keeping tabs on me good, but I don't think she expected me to find my faith again. I mean after all, Lucifer once had wings too. The more Matt rejected me the more that pushed me towards Andy. Night after night, weekend after weekend, it started blending into each other. Those months went by so fast. When I look back, so much happened in such a short period. Sometimes my mind gets delirious trying to recapture the timeline of events. I try hard to remember just where and when things happened, but honestly, you can't remember everything in a sequence when your mind is so gone. Although I remember the last time Matt and I were together, because Andy was there. I finally got my wish, it was that sick and disturbed wish I had wanted to come true since Matt had cheated on me with Crisita. I thought by making this wish come true, some way, somehow Matt would feel the pain I had in my soul. I still harbored pain no matter how many lines I snorted, drinks I drank and pills I popped. I can't remember what date it was, but I do remember what month it was. It was July 2016 and it was just a week later, that what was left of the rest my world, would start it's last decent into the darkest most unforgiving hell I would ever see.

Andy, Matt and I had once again had been partying for days. Andy and I broke free from Matt for a little bit in the morning after his gig and we were sitting around the house once again getting high and as luck would have it, I found the LSD that Matt had forgotten about. It was Sweet Tarts candy laced with drops of LSD that Matt purchased from Rick a while back and stupidly left at my house when he moved out and left me there with Andy. Matt didn't care about anything but drugs and having sex with other women so I suppose he forgot to take his drugs with him when he moved out because he was in a rush to get to another woman. That's cool though, cause now I had his acid. I started giggling about that and popped one into my mouth. When I walked out to the porch, this other guy had showed up. His name was David and what a character he was. A nice guy so it seemed, but a real character. He was short and really just a funny little guy with brown mousey hair and a crazy little look in his hazy blue eyes. I swear every one of these people in my life has blue eyes and although I can't figure out what the connection is I suppose someday God will reveal this to me. His brother was a very well-known musician in a national touring band and well, he bought cocaine from me on occasion so I suppose he was alright. I sat in my chair and stared right into Andy's eyes while David babbled on about something. I had a big smirk on my face. Andy looked back at me smiling with a "what's up" look on his face. Andy knew something was up. I mouthed the word "acid" to him and let me just tell you, I saw the brightest smile on a man's face that you could ever see. I was tripping my ass off but there was only one Sweet Tart left, and it was going to be Andy's.

I whispered to him, "You want one?"

"Hell yeah, I do."

So, with that we left David outside on the back porch alone and babbling to himself, I fetched the acid laced Sweet Tart. Andy tried to take it from me, but no way. I was going to put it into his mouth. I placed the Sweet Tart on his tongue as he closed his mouth around my fingers.

"How much do you love me know?" I asked him.

"I love you a whole hell of a lot. More than I did last night and not quite as much as I will tomorrow, or rather 10 minutes from now." he said.

"Oh Andy, you are going to adore me for the next *seventeen hours!*" I responded with an evil giggle.

"Seventeen hours?"

"Yup! That's how long that trip is going to last." I said with such satisfaction. And so, the trip began.

Matt ended up coming over but we didn't tell him we just dropped his acid. He was coked out of his mind anyway but I honestly didn't notice at first. I remember having to follow David home because he bought cocaine from me. He only had twenty dollars on him, and he owed me more money so we decided I was going to get paid the rest in weed. That was okay too because I would have to smoke it to get to sleep as I was out of Xanax. Geez, just writing that makes me want to vomit. To think I put that much poison into my body is unbelievable. What was I thinking? That's just it, I wasn't thinking. I was only fixated on where the next high was going to come from and how I was going to get my peace. I made Matt drive with David because I didn't trust him. Besides, I wanted Andy in my car. We were both tripping on the same plateau and it was awesome. I didn't need Matt bringing me down while I was trying to drive while tripping. Again, the things I did that could've potentially killed me, or worse yet, that I could've hurt someone else, is unimaginable to me now. It wasn't until after I got clean that I sat down and thought about all the potential tragedy that could've occurred while I was messed up. You don't think when you are like that, with any logic or reason at all. You think you are invincible, like you are this immortal god, that nothing can touch you or hurt you. I suppose that's why I did what I did. It was the only time in my life that I ever felt wanted and loved. Damn, I just wanted to be enough. Even if it was for just one person, I wanted to be the one that they adored and that they couldn't live without. That's what the drugs did for me. The drugs loved me and I loved them right back. They made me number one and in turn I gave drugs every bit of my life, my soul and my worth. In the end, it was nothing but a façade; another disappointment and another false quest to be accepted.

***

When Andy, Matt and I got back, we went to Matts house and the games began. Andy and I were sitting by the pool and laughing and giggling like two little kids enjoying our trip while Matt looked on at us in a questioning way. When they disappeared to Matts room to do a line, I got this crazy idea to put *my* plan in motion. I walked straight into Matts room and stripped down in front of them. I climb into Matt's bed and laid there with my elbow propping me up. Their mouths open to the floor.

"Andy, I do believe Christina wants us to fuck her." Matt said.

"Hum," Andy said thinking, "well I suppose we should make her fantasy come true."

"No Matt, for right now, I'd like you to sit in that chair over there in the corner and watch how Andy fucks me. Maybe you can learn something for the next girl you cheat on me with."

Andy looked at Matt and confirmed that we had been together before this was about to happen.

"So, you two have already been together?"

"Yeah, we have." Andy confessed, "Now let me show you how she likes it."

So, Andy did just that. He showed Matt how to make me feel like I was everything – that I was enough all while Matt sat in that chair watching. I laid on my back in anticipation of Andy. He crawled on the bed like a male panther ready to devour his prey. As he hovered over me and kissed me thoroughly on the lips he plunged his tongue into my mouth and suddenly, I didn't see Matt in the room. Andy's hand caressed my body and made me feel alive in my horribly dead world. His touch lit me on fire light a blaze running rampant through a house that was completely out of control. His hands explored my body and slowly down my waist and to my thighs. His arms wrapped so tight around me, lifting me up, guiding my body down onto him as he penetrated me deeply. Oh, my God he was so deep inside me. I let out a cry as he rocked me back and forth, never letting me go, keeping his tongue firmly inside my mouth. As he made love to me, he continued to work his tongue down my neck all the way up to the top of my chest. I leaned my head back in awe of the craziness he made me feel inside. As my back arched backwards, he kneeled up while still inside of me, bringing my hips up as high as they could go to reach his thrusting. He took me on a wild ride as lightning poured out of me while two bodies became one in our cries for each other's pleasure. Matt never made me feel like that. The things that Andy made me feel were amazing. It was like being in a field of dreams with each one of them coming true. After a while, we had Matt join us, and then he took the lesson that Andy gave him on how to make love to me and threw it right out the window! I was disappointed to say the least! Matt began to pound me with all the anger he had in his soul. Andy stopped Matt almost immediately and told him to get the hell out of his room. This was a nice surprise, to see Andy like this. While he cleaned me up, he held me and he spoke softly to me.

"Matt's to rough with you, Christina. I don't like how he does that to you and neither should you. I will never treat you like that. You should be cherished, not fucked like an animal."

"Sex is just sex to Matt, Andy. Even after 3 years, that's still all it is to him." I said with my face buried into Andy's neck.

***

My body hurt so bad from how Matt manhandled me I couldn't help but weep. Even the tears that were rolling down my face hurt. I was in so much pain but Andy was there to take that pain away. I loved Matt, but my god he had hurt me repeatedly over the years and I was over it. Up until then, I would have done anything for him. I guess now in my sobriety, I realized it's called being co-dependent. I didn't know how to be any other way. It was like being with ex-husband number two all over again. Only the abuse was in a different way. Purely mental abuse and after that episode, I suppose you would call it some sort of sexual abuse. But I was the one who got naked in front of them so in essence, I asked for it. Another flawless mistake thoroughly thought out. After Andy saw the violent love - making, he wanted to protect me and be with me even more.

"Stay here until I fall asleep. Please?", I asked.

"I'm not going anywhere. I won't leave you. I love you." He acted so convincing, and besides I was already so tired and the acid and all the coke we had done had finally taken its toll on me. My body shut down and once again, I found some sort of peace once the world became dark around me. The only time I had peace was when I was sleeping. It was like being dead. You don't dream when you are on drugs. There are no dreams, no nightmares, no feelings, no emotions. You are essentially dead when you sleep. You are up for days on end and then finally, your body gives out and you succumb to the dark abyss of sleep. This is where nothing can hurt us. This is where we are at peace.

About six hours later, I woke up in Matts bed, still sore after the thrashing Matt gave me. I was still confused and out of sorts from the acid alone, feeling like I did sure didn't help. I thought to myself no matter how steamy I thought that whole thing was, it was so not like me. Was I in a nightmare or did this happen? That's what drugs will do, make you think you're queen of the night! Then suddenly, I snapped out of it and realized it was true. Everything I thought was a nightmare was true. Holy crap! At forty-six years old, I had a threesome. Wow. Oh man, was I going downhill fast.

There weren't enough brake pads left to stop me. I was like a 1984 Fierro sliding sideways down a hill on ice in the middle of winter on a Pennsylvania back road. Then, I smelled food. I couldn't remember the last time I ate. When was the last time I was home? I had two dogs and two cats at home and when was the last time I saw them? I couldn't remember anything except what took place in that bedroom earlier that afternoon. It was now six o'clock on a Sunday and I had to get prepared for work for the next day. But I needed to eat first so I got up and walked out to the living room where Matt and Andy were playing acoustic guitar.

"Hey sleepy head." Andy said with a crooked smile.

"Hey", I said with a groggy undertone, "where's the food I am so hungry."

"There isn't any left. You missed it because you were a party pooper and slept all day so you don't get to eat." Matt said in a nasty voice.

"Dude, why you got to be so mean to her. She's hungry." Andy said like a proud boyfriend. That's my hero. Having come down from the acid, I was irritable and starving, and quite pissed!

"Fuck you Matt!" I started to flip. "Go find your whores and go cook dinner for them. You railroad my body like you think it's a fucking machine and then deny me food? You're a sadistic asshole! I'm out of here. I'm going home! I'm done with you and I can't take it anymore being with you. You cheat, you lie and all these cunts you cheat on me with get treated better than me! Fuck you!" I screamed at the top of my lungs.

***

Then just like that, I walked out the door, got in my car and went home. I was never with Matt again. Even though he treated me like shit, I sometimes still think about him and I get sad. I truly loved him for a while, even though he was abusive. We used to have a lot of fun before that night we got our first gram of cocaine. We would cook Italian Sunday dinners together and he'd put on some old swing music or old brat pack music. Sometimes Frank Sinatra would be blasting on Pandora singing *'Come Fly with Me'* and he'd grab me away from the stove while cooking the penne pasta and danced with me through the kitchen- old ballroom style- and I'd giggle and laugh at how bad of a dancer he was until I had tears in my eyes and my tummy hurt from laughing. I miss laughing like that sometimes. But I loved him, for all the cheating and hurt he put me through, I still loved him. For the few happy stolen moments, Matt made me feel alive. It wasn't a lot of the time I spent him, but for a few brief moments I knew what it felt like to laugh. I long someday to find that again with someone. Not the bad stuff, but someone who will dance with me in the kitchen; someone who makes my heart feel so full and wonderful. Someone who makes me laugh until I can't catch my breath. Someone I love and someone to love me back unconditionally. That day I left Matt standing in his living room was the day I decided I needed peace and very soon.

Andy decided to come to my house a few minutes after I left, walking through my front door without knocking. He was quiet as he knew I was hurting. I suppose hearing me sobbing in my bedroom with face buried in my pillows on my bed gave it away. He climbed onto the bed gently, wrapping his body me and around me and held me while I cried, and cried and cried some more. It felt like that my tears would never end. I knew that was the last time I was to see Matt. I knew the Matt I once loved wasn't there anymore. I knew the woman he once loved was gone too. As I turned to Andy and laid my head on his chest with his arms wrapped around me, I looked up into his eyes.

"What's up sweetheart?", he asked with empathy.

"I have something to ask you", I responded in a shaky voice.

"What's that?"

I took a deep breath.

"If I asked you to shoot me up, would you?"

"You want me to shoot you up?"

"Yeah."

"Why?"

"I want to feel your peace. You come out of my bathroom every time with this amazing look of peace on your face. I want to feel peace like that."

"Christina, you need to understand something; shooting up is unlike any high you have ever felt. Once you do it, I will guarantee you that you will never snort it, eat it or put it on your gums ever again. Are you ready for that? Do really want that?"

Looking straight into Andy's eyes and with determination, I said, "I'm ready. I need your peace. I want to feel your peace. But I want you to do it for me. I can't do it myself."

"Ok. Only on one condition."

"What's that?"

"Promise me you will never let anyone shoot you up but me. You must be careful who you trust when you get into this world. I also don't want you doing it without me around. I don't want anyone shooting you up except me. Promise me that and I'll do it."

"I promise. I will never do it unless you are with me."

"Ok. When do you want to do it?"

"Friday night? Next Friday night."

"Done, it's a date."

***

All week I was on edge. Andy and I planned this first high so it would be perfect in every way. We sold a lot of cocaine that week to make a lot of money so we could afford a lot of cocaine for Friday night. We stayed clean that whole week so I would feel the full effect. He suggested the dry-out period to prepare my body and my blood to experience the full effect of the boot. As I've said numerous times, every grand mistake I ever made was always thoroughly thought out and perfectly executed. However, since then I have found out that the prime way to experience an overdose is to do exactly that. Nine out of 10 overdoses happen when a person has been dried out or they have never shot up before. What I did the week before by drying out thinking that it was going to be perfectly executed could in fact have killed me then. I had almost put myself in a grave by adhering to Andy's suggestion. When Friday night came, I raced home across the Veterans Memorial Bridge after work because there was preparation to be had. I wanted everything perfect. My surroundings had to be perfect. The hot tub had to be ready for when we got home so the first thing I did was feed my dogs and the cats and then turn the hot tub on. The bubbles were beautiful, and as I stood there and pictured me and Andy on the same level of high hanging out in the bubbling water and enjoying each other's company, I felt peaceful. I went inside and began primping myself to look stunning for the evening. I wanted the night to be absolutely perfect. I put on my favorite jeans and tank top with my favorite black boots. I was now a size two, skin and bones and pretty much a walking skeleton. Just a shadow of the woman I once was. I was getting ready for the evening like I was going to attend the Oscars for crying out loud! Andy came home and as I was racing around the house in my preparations, he asked me, "Are you ready for tonight?"

"Yes!" I said quickly with a silly school girl giggle. "I'm so excited!"

As I watched Andy get dressed and ready for the evening, I asked, "You're still ok with booting me up, right? You're not going to let me down, are you? Please don't let me down Andy."

"Have I let you down yet?"

"No."

"Then why would you ask me a silly question like that?"

"I don't know. Stupid, right? I should know better. You always protect me and always have my back."

"Damn straight I do woman! Now let's go out and make this a night to remember."

I had a smile on my face and the dark side of my soul prepared for the night. However, this was something no one could be ready for. What I thought was going to be the best night of my life, was going to become the beginning of the worst journey of my life.

We went to Matts gig for a little bit and then I started getting antsy. I didn't want to be there anymore and Andy could see it. I didn't want to watch

Matt and the older woman sitting at the bar again make secret smiling faces at each other. Andy and I were so in tune to each other he could feel my anxiety. He came up to me after finishing his conversation with some friends and asked me if I was ready to go. Holy cow, was I ever. As we were walking out, Matt stopped us and asked where we were going.

I wanted to hurt Matt for hurting me so I simply said close to his ear, "I'm going home with Andy so I can feel his peace." I stared dead into Matts eyes with no expression whatsoever. I already felt numbness sweep over me. I saw tears well up in his eyes. Until this day, I think Matt knew exactly what I was about to do that night. But he never made any effort to stop me. I keep thinking that if he would've just told me he loved me and for once during that time had shown me that he loved me and cared about me. I wonder if I would've not fallen down the path that was in front of me. Both paths sucked. I'm sure it wouldn't have mattered that night or not. All I know now is what happens right now. The decisions I make now have consequences that I am aware of, good or bad. My decisions back then where the decisions of an addict in active addiction. Living for one thing no matter what the consequences were. I was immortal. Looking at Matt in the frame of mind I was in back then, I was immortal. For what I was about to do, there was going to be peace in my life and I'd live forever. Matt wouldn't be able to hurt me anymore. My dad wouldn't be able to be a sorrowful memory anymore. My mother's death wouldn't hurt anymore. The fact that I didn't have my music or Rob or my sister in my life anymore couldn't hurt me again and to top it all off, I was going to be enough. *I was going to be enough.*

***

Andy and I went home followed by a couple of friends that were going to buy cocaine off of me. When we walked in the door my heart began to race. I knew my world as I knew it then was somehow going to go on the most fantastic ride of my life, although I had no idea what to expect. I changed into my shorts and a t-shirt and directed the customers into my room to purchase their goods. Andy stayed in the doorway propped against the molding waiting for me. As I grabbed our stash, which was the good stuff and not the stuff I sold to customers, I walked up to Andy and gazed into his eyes. Breaking the gaze, Andy said, "Guys, Christina and I will be right back. Make yourselves at home." I followed Andy into the bathroom. He closed the door and locked it. He gestured to me to pour some cocaine out into the bottle cap that had been carefully prepared with a bit of cotton in it. I emptied a good amount into the cap and then he drew 40 CC's of water into the syringe and squirted it into the bottle cap and mixed the cocaine and water together. He took his belt off and told me to wrap it around my upper arm. As I did this, he drew the liquidized cocaine into the needle. I was in awe as I knew that the liquid would soon be running through my veins.

"Andy, where should I sit? Where would be easiest for you? Have you ever done this to someone before?" I was nervous and a complete chatter box.

"Yes, I have. But I have never done it to someone being their first time. I'm scared and I'm nervous. But even more so because it's you I'm doing it to."

"Don't be nervous. You're my hero, you're giving me my peace. Now, where should I sit?

"Sit on the floor. Just in case something happens."

"OK", I said enthusiastically as I sat on the floor.

"Now, turn your arm out and keep pumping your hand into a fist until I tell you to stop, just like at the doctor when they draw blood."

"Oh, I can totally do that!" I said excitedly. My veins started to plump up. I never noticed how healthy my veins were before.

Andy found the vein in the crook of my arm. Before he went for it he looked at me.

"Are you ready?"

"Yeah, I'm ready" I said in a whisper.

With that, he pushed the needle into my vein. It was the most excruciating yet beautiful pain I've ever felt. He drew the plunger back and I watched as my dark red blood entered the syringe. He told me to hold completely still and I did. He pushed the plunger down into the syringe. I watched the liquid cocaine mixed with my blood disappear into my arm.

"Now, unwrap the tourniquet slowly." Andy said never taking his eyes off the needle that was still in my arm.

I slowly removed his belt as he pulled the needle out of my arm, very slowly. A little bit of blood came out of the puncture and I licked it as I saw him do on many occasions. Andy counted three, two, one and then it happened. It felt like a tidal wave hitting the beach with all its power with a thunderstorm raging the surf. Bolts of lightning I could feel running through my veins so fast and out of control. My world was on the most outrageous roller coaster ride I'd ever been on and I was the conductor. I was Alice on this glorious beautiful trip through Wonderland and I had the White Rabbit right next to me every step of the way. It hit my mouth with the most unbelievable taste. My mouth immediately got numb, tasting like that liquid metal only 1000% more intensified. Like a sparkling rush of sweet tasting glitter on my tongue. Then it immediately hit my eyes and faster than lightning went right to my head. I lift my head up and looked into Andy's eyes and with a gasp of breath I couldn't believe what I was feeling. Andy stayed kneeling in front of me with a smile across his face, as if he was looking at an angel.

"Oh my God. You're flying."

"Really! This is what it feels like? Oh my God! Andy it's beautiful! It's like everything around me is beautiful! I can hear everything. I can hear your heart beating!"

"I told you it would be. You okay?"

"Yes. I'm so okay. Thank you. Thank you for giving me my peace."

"You're welcome. Just promise me you will never let anyone do this to you but me"

"I promise. I love you Andy. Thank you so much."

Andy, kissed me with his eyes and lips, penetrating my soul like no other. I was experiencing pure bliss and I loved it.

"Come on. Can you stand up?"

"I don't know."

"Come on, I'll help you. I won't let you go." Andy helped me to my up and told me to look in the mirror.

"What do you see?"

"My eyes! They're beautiful! They're huge and black as night!" I said still thrashing from the initial high. "I can't see the green in my eyes!"

My smile was *huge*! I finally had peace. It was the most beautiful thing I've ever seen or felt in myself.

Then Andy shot himself up. Then me again. We were finally on the same plateau, the ultimate high. All the pain and hurt was gone. It vanished. I felt complete bliss. Andy shot us both up all night long. Every time he shot me up, he'd kiss me afterwards. As the night went on, we got into some deep conversations.

"Thank you for being my peace Andy. You *are* my peace."

"And you're my peace." he said back at me with love in his eyes.

"It's like, I had this incredible pain inside and you took it all away. Ya know like, when the needle goes into me, it reminds me of the pain that Matt has given me and then I watch you push the plunger down on my arm and you are the one that delivers my peace to my body. Inside me. Does that make sense?"

"It makes perfect sense."

"Good. Now let's shoot up again."

And so, we did. And every time Andy shot me up, more and more of my pain and my hurt and my memories of the past and of not being enough, slowly faded away.

***

Andy was right. I never snorted, ate or gummed cocaine again. In fact, I bought needles at a pharmacy in town that sold them with no problem.

Andy and I would share needles when we got low and couldn't make it to the pharmacy. It was okay I thought as he assured me he didn't have diseases or issues and I believed him because he said I was his best friend, his home. Why on earth would you put someone's life in danger that you love. For six weeks that's all we did. I would come home from work and we would shoot up all night long. We would go days without food or sleep. Andy never got a job but somehow, someway every day I made it to work. I was an engineering project manager for a glass company. I was a professional making my way in the world and I was successful. I could handle being messed up for four days and then close a deal at work with no problem. And as that delusion kept going on, the bruises started showing on my arms. I would walk into work in shorts and flip flops because I had no clean clothes. I would fall asleep at my desk. I started bringing cocaine to work and trying to shoot myself up, but without Andy, I couldn't get high. It hurt so much when I couldn't get high. So much for the pain disappearing. Andy would sleep all day while I was at work and then expect me to party all night long. He kept me up for days and days shooting me up. Then the paranoia set in and my mind started to play tricks on me. Andy saw this and used it to his advantage. He used the fact of my mind slipping to get what he wanted. He would read articles about paranoia to me while I was high and locked in the bathroom with him. He would convince me that I was seeing things. People were stealing from me. People were now in my house that I didn't know. Girls that I didn't know that were junkies and that played along with Andy and convinced me there was dope hiding in light sockets and my plants out on my porch. I would tear everything apart looking for things that Andy said people stole from me. When all it was, was an illustrious playing of my mind that Andy would do while he was the one stealing from me. Lucifer's messenger had snared my foot and was not going to let go until he destroyed me. Again, doing drugs had now made me into a delusional mess. I believed things that weren't true. I saw things that weren't there. I trusted people that should've never been trusted. Shooting cocaine turned into shooting other drugs as well. Crack, OxyContin and Dilauded were the IV drugs of choice at my house. My house was now called "The Crack House" and rightly so.

***

It wasn't always bad. Andy was loving sometimes. Especially the times when he was getting the cocaine from his dealer and getting high while he was shooting me up with water. He would use all of it himself and switch the needles. I found out later from David that Andy would always keep a needle filled with water and just a little bit of cocaine in it for me and he would switch it just before he would puncture my skin. I got wise to this after a while and decided to hold my own bag of dope so I could get high with the hundreds of dollars that I was spending every week. The morning of September 12th, 2016, I went into work in my usual tank top, shorts and flip flops. I had been up all weekend long. I had bruises all up and down my arms that I didn't care about. It was almost like I was proud of them. I was high as a kite with a lot of cocaine on me because I couldn't leave it at home anymore. Andy would do it all before I got home and then it would cost me more money to get high that night. Besides, I couldn't get high without Andy administering it. It was impossible for me to shoot myself up. So many times, I tried but I couldn't do it.

The boss' assistant, we'll call her Crystal, came into my office and told me it was my last day. I didn't cause a scene. I knew why. I started packing up all my stuff and just then the boss lady walked in.

"Packing up all your shit?"

"Yeah, yeah I am."

"Good. I think it's for the best. Don't you?"

"Absolutely." And with that, I got in my car and left. I didn't feel bad at all. I had about $100 on me so I went to the pharmacy that sold the needles, bought a package, and continued my way home.

When I got home, Andy called from my bedroom where he was taking his usual slumber.

"Christina, is that you?"

"Yeah."

"What are you doing home?", Andy asked.

I went in the room and sat on the bed in a half lotus yoga position.

"I got fired."

"Ok. You alright?"

"Yeah. Surprisingly, I'm good with it."

"What do you want to do?"

Andy knew exactly what I wanted to do.

"I want to get high. And I want to be totally high."

"Well then," Andy contorted, "I've always been taught to give a woman exactly what she wants. Come on sweetheart, let's go get you high."

***

So, there I was once again, in the darkest places of my mind. The most horrible dreadful existence known to me had become the one thing I lived for. The ultimate beautiful high. In the dark reaches of my heart and my mind, I knew this was all wrong but how do I stop? How do I turn back the hands of time? How do I live now? I lived for the moments Andy would puncture my rotting skin and my failing veins with that needle. It only took eight weeks to destroy my life. I was now the junkie that I had once seen and despised when I lived in New York. I would watch the homeless drug addicts shoot up in dark alleys and even though I would try to help them by bringing them food and blankets and delivering clean needles through the Needle Exchange of New York when I was at Julliard, I despised the fact that I had now become one of them. David came to my house from North Fort Myers and joined us in getting high. He had a prescription for Dilauded and some crack on him. I'd never done crack until I start shooting up with Andy. It was a decent high but crack you don't dilute it with water. You must dilute it with vinegar. The vinegar burns when it's first administered. It sets your veins on fire. If the crack is well made, it travels through your veins quickly and straight to your heart. I did it a couple of times that Monday. I did a back to back dosage. Andy shot me up with 40cc's of crack first and then piggy backed it with 60cc's of cocaine. I had no idea what was about to happen. All I wanted was to be higher than I ever was before and I wanted that high to last forever if it could. But I wasn't prepared for the bells. The Bells! The Bells! It was like St. Patrick's Cathedral is going off in my head! My body went completely numb. I turned to look at Andy but couldn't hear anything but the bells in my ears. They were so loud. So deafeningly loud. My legs went numb. My head and my mind were even numbed. As I felt the floor drop out beneath me, I felt his beautiful tattooed arms encase me as I fell to the floor; all the while Andy was holding me staring into my eyes.

"Don't you die on me, Christina? Christina! Look at me! Christina, breathe! Don't you dare die on me!" he said with conviction in his voice. I heard him yelling at me. I could hear his heart beating. I could hear him blinking his eyes. I could hear everything in high definition sound. As I laid there on the floor in Andy's arms in my living room, I could see a man, standing in front of me. There was an extreme golden bright light behind him which lined out a black silhouette. As he walked towards me, I recognized him as my father, Joe. He held out his hand and lifted me up off the floor, out of Andy's grasp. He felt safe and he felt warm with that bright golden light surrounding the both of us. He made the bells go away. He hugged me and stroked my hair in a calming manner. Oh I didn't want this to end. This was peace. This was the peace that I had longed for and it was beautiful. It was quiet and serene. There was nothing like it on earth and I wanted to stay there with him. But my Dad had other plans and I think God did too. My Dad pushed me back slowly to look at me. As I peered into my father's blue eyes, I realized how young and healthy he looked. He was bathed in what I can only explain as grace and glory. I turned to look down at my body lying in Andy's arms. As I turned back to my Dad I said, "Daddy take me with you, please take me with you!" He looked at me with such sadness in his eyes, but in an understanding way. As a tear rolled down his face he said to me with a slight smile, "Not yet Chrissy. Not yet." He put me back in Andy's arms, looking at me lovingly, nodding his head as he faded away

***

The bells in my head were still slightly ringing, and instead of that safe warm place with my Dad, I looked around and realized I was lying on the floor in my living room. This is where there was no living whatsoever. My beautiful little apartment had turned into a crack house. All there was were needles, drugs and fucked up people scattered about, using my house as a facility to get high in. When I finally came to, I knew I had to get out of there but I wanted to hear the bells again. I wanted to see my dad again. I wanted him to take me with him, so I chased that high for three more days. Every time Andy shot me up with more and more cocaine, every time he stuck the needle into my arm and pushed the plunger down, I prayed to hear those bells again. His favorite place to shoot me up was in the crook of my right arm. He never missed there. We were feigning, like hungry zombies that couldn't get enough flesh to eat. Every time Andy got me high, he would look at me lovingly to make sure I got the hit. I could feel the liquidized cocaine run through my veins, then it would hit my tongue with that beautiful taste, finally, ending in my head. I would smack my lips together from the taste while gazing into Andy's eyes. We always locked eyes together every single time he mainlined me and would smile at me in amazement as to how beautiful I looked as the high was battering me. Then he would kiss me and tell me he loved me. It was a bond we shared together. He took away my pain, he gave me peace and he always said I was enough for him. In return, I gave him my heart, my soul and my life. The bells, however, never rang again, and on that third day, my world as I knew it for the past 8 months had come to a screeching halt. That 3rd day was the first day of the rest of my life.

I made the gravest of mistakes and I later paid the price for the mistake that I now owned.

CHRISTINA GIORDANO

CHAPTER 9

THE MAGNIFICENT SEVEN

***

Then the seven angels who had the seven trumpets prepared to sound them. The first angel sounded his trumpet, and there came hail and fire mixed with blood, and it was hurled down to earth. ~ *Revelation 8:6-7*

I've learned the term *Rock Bottom* means jail, institution or death. It's that very pinnacle point when you find out exactly who loves you unconditionally and who could care less if you lived or died in their arms. I found that unconditional love in seven people. Cindy Vaughn, Anne Marie Lago, Matt Vananyek, Kimberly Bigelow, Celeste Mollica, Brent Legere and of course, my best friend of forty-three years, Cheryl. It was September 14th, 2016 when my world came to a crashing halt and stood still. It was the third day after that incredible bell ringing high and looking around my beautiful little apartment destroyed, made me disgusted. There were people sitting in my living room shooting up, people in my kitchen shooting up, in the bathroom, in my bedroom, people sitting at my dining room table shooting up. I went to my room and kicked everyone out, sat on my bed and began to cry. I had three hundred dollars to my name hidden ironically in my Bible, rent was due in a week, I couldn't remember the last time I saw or fed my two little old Chihuahuas or my two cats.

My life as I knew it, was over. It spiraled down a dark dreaded hole so fast I couldn't crawl out of it. Even if I wanted to crawl out I didn't have the first clue how I was going to do it. I was in hook, line and sinker. And it sucked. Andy had just shot me up with crack cocaine while I simultaneously collided with a fierce dose of reality. I had this strange, ethereal and powerful feeling that sort of made my high not so good. I was in a dark rabbit hole that engulfed me. Every fiber of my being was destroyed. Then, Andy came in to my room with the biggest smile on his face, speaking in an evil satanic voice that would've made the devil proud.

"What's the matter Christina?"

"Andy, I'm going to lose everything."

"Ha-ha! Yeah you sure are. Welcome to my world Christina. You are now a full-fledged junkie!"

"What are you saying Andy?" I said freaking out.

"I'm saying I'm glad. I finally destroyed your life. You think all that was real? Everything I said was true? Ha-ha! You aren't as smart as you think you are. I got exactly what I wanted from you and more. Now you're a pathetic addict and I'm the only one that can shoot you up because you can't do it yourself. All I would have do now is turn you out and make some money off you. That's the way the game works sweetheart. I played the fuck out of you."

I sat there on my bed high and in shock. The little bit of self-worth I thought I had was ripped away and exposed. Andy walked over to my Bible, opened it and took one hundred and eighty dollars to buy more cocaine, like he was entitled to the small amount of money I had left to my name. When he walked out, I instantly felt the biggest rush of evil envelop around me. It was the darkest most evil feeling I've ever felt; like Lucifer was consoling me. Satan's messengers were walking around my house in human form and all his minions were scattered about my house. I gathered the rest of the cash from my Bible, walked out into my living room that was filled with pure evil and grabbed my phone, my iPad, my computer, my purse and my car keys. Then I ran out of my house in a t-shirt and panties, jumped into my car and took off. Leaving everything behind. The only one I could think of calling was Cindy Vaughn. Cindy was known in our music scene as a 'bad ass bitch' and I was glad that we were friends. She is a beautiful woman inside and out with long gorgeous black hair that has turquoise, blue and purple streaks through it. Her eyes, wouldn't you know it are blue. She's a tour manager for national rock music acts and she's tough as nails. You never catch her out on the town without being dressed to the nines and she can rock a corset like no other woman I know. Pair that with a leather jacket, tight jeans and stiletto knee high boots and you have the ultimate rock and roll chick. I was on the bad side of her once and I didn't like being there. Cindy is the type of friend that I'll call a 'warrior friend'. If she loves you she will not hesitate to put on the gauntlets and fight for you. She also had her dealings with Andy stealing from her so I knew she would listen to me vent. Although, I didn't call her for a pep talk, I called her because I needed someone to save my life. She lived way out in no man's land, Arcadia, Florida, without any cell phone signal so I didn't know if she would even pick up. I dialed her number as I was whispering to myself, "Cindy please, please pick up the phone." I was high as a kite and I was driving aimlessly around town.

"Hey girl, what's happening?" her voice was the voice of my first angel that entered my darkness to rescue me.

I screamed and cried into the phone, "Cindy, help me please! I don't know what to do. He's got me I'm hooked on shooting up. I've been shooting up for about two months now and I can't do it anymore. I don't remember the last time I fed my Chihuahuas or my cats, I've been up for 3 days straight shooting up, I lost my job and I can't get him and all the other people out of my apartment! Help me, please! I don't know what to do! I'm not strong enough anymore!"

"Hold on baby, where are you?"

"I don't know! I'm driving around Cape Coral in my car. I'm high as a kite, Andy just shot me up with crack and I don't know what I'm doing or where I'm going. Cindy please come get me! I have to stop doing this and I don't know how!"

"Christina, what does he have you on? Can you make it home? I am coming to get you. And, I will get Andy out of your house! Mark my words because it's not going to be pretty and it's not going to be subtle. I am going to rain fire on his world! Party time is over and if he's smart he will heed my warning."

"He's shooting me up with cocaine, crack, oxy and dilauded! I'm snorting Xanax for Christ sake! You name the drug and he's got me on it! I'm scared I'm going to die. I think I can make it home but Cindy, I don't want to go in that house but my 2 little old girls are in there and so are Natasha and Ace! I can't believe I left them in there with all those junkies in my house! Oh my God! I have to get home! They're probably so scared! I'm so scared Cindy please help me!"

"Okay, listen to me. Is Brent home? If he is, go there now. If he's not, stay in your car in your driveway. Lock the car doors and wait for me."

"Ok. Ok I will."

"Okay, honey. I love you Christina, I'm on my way."

"Okay."

When we hung up, I started screaming uncontrollably like a crazy person. I was completely gone. My mind was gone. My life was gone. Then suddenly, I started sobbing and I felt like a lost little girl who needed her mommy and daddy. I was crying for help this whole time and every one of my friends knew it but me. I wanted my mom and dad so bad right now. I hurt so much. That pain was the worst pain. My heart hurt, my mind hurt, my bones and muscles felt like they were dead. But most all, my spirit was in the most unbelievably mortifying state it could ever bear. My spirit died somewhere and somehow and now I wondered how I was ever going to come back and put my body, mind and soul back together. It wasn't because of what Andy said. It wasn't like losing a boyfriend or a loved one. I lost myself. I lost the woman I once knew. I lost the hateful and powerful Christina and became the little girl again waving goodbye to her best friend from the back seat of her parent's car. I was the little girl who wasn't good enough for the first chair flute in the high school band. I was the girl who lost the love of her life when he shot himself in the head a month before she was supposed to marry him. Then, I saw myself as the girl who was throwing the Bibles at the crucifixion above the alter in the Catholic church when her mother died. All the pain and all the hurt came crashing in all at once. I started driving faster and faster just so I could get to safety. I wanted to feel safe again I wanted my life back again. I realized the grave mistake I made and I owned it from the beginning. I called Denise after I got off the phone with Cindy. I told her what was going on and she stayed on the phone with me for the whole ride back to my place.

I made it home without killing anybody and thank goodness Brent's Jeep was in the parking lot. Brent is my next-door neighbor and a good friend. I tease Brent a lot about being the "sexy neighbor dude". He's always walking around with his shirt off, in a pair of jeans and bare feet like some kind of BDSM character from an erotic novel. He's got long light brown hair, ripped up muscles and beautiful, hazel eyes that would melt any girls heart. His actual heart holds a lot of love for his friends and the people that he's close to. I experienced that love and kindness from him that day and every day after that. He's the second angel of *The Magnificent Seven*, for without him answering his door when I got back to my apartment, I would've had to go inside my house and probably would've had Andy shoot me up again.

I pull into the parking lot and ran to his door which is next to mine and banged on it with my fist so furiously. I could hear Andy in my apartment through the thin walls walking to the door. I knocked on Brent's door in panic mode and then as I heard Andy approaching I started yelling. "Brent! Brent! Open the door, open your door please! Let me in!"

Both my apartment door and Brent's door opened at the same time and as Andy was reaching for me, I flew passed by Brent into his apartment, pleading with him the whole time to shut door and to not let Andy in. Brent, the stud he was, put his hand up in front of Andy's chest.

"That's far enough buddy."

"I need to talk to Christina now. She's upset and I'm worried about her." Andy said trying to convince Brent that he cared.

"Well, she needs a little bit of space right now obviously so let me talk to her first."

"Ok man, please tell her I care about her."

With that, Brent shut door and came over to me. I explained to him in the voice of a crazy strung out junkie what had happened. I told him Cindy was coming to get me and that I couldn't get Andy out of my house.

"Christina, I knew something wasn't right over there. I knew about the drugs and I knew about you shooting up. It was obvious. But I didn't know he was the one shooting you up. I don't like him and I never did."

"I know, I know" I said in a pleading voice. "Brent, I'm so sorry. You knew? I'm so tired and my head is spinning. I didn't know what to do. Cindy told me to come here."

"Good! Your safe here. I'm not going to let him hurt you anymore. This is enough and it needs to stop today. I love you so much and it kills me every day to know that I couldn't help you until you made that decision."

"How did you know?"

"Christina! Look at your arms! You are covered in bruises! Your arms and your feet are torn up!"

I looked down at my arms to see the mess I had made of my skin. My arms were bruised; purple, black and blue marks running up and down my arms and my feet. Oh, my God! What did I do to myself? My body and my mind was so damaged. All I could seem to do was cry because that's the only emotion I knew. Complete sorrow took over me and all Brent could do was sit on the bed and hold me. It felt comforting to finally be held by someone who cared, who loved me and who genuinely knew me for the woman I used to be, not the mess I had become.

I heard Cindy's car pull up. She has a brand new Camaro. It wouldn't matter how high a person is, you can always recognize the sound of a Camaro. Brent went to the door and opened it. In walked my "warrior friend".

She ran right over to me and sat on the bed and held me and rocked me back and forth like a child. I was so lost. She was strong for me when I couldn't be. She grabbed my shoulders and looked into my sad, teary eyes and said, "Are you ready for this, because this isn't going to be easy. First, I'm going to get that mother fucker out of your house and then I'm taking you and the girls out to my house where no one can contact you where you're going to dry out." Then she saw my arms and began to cry. "Oh honey, my beautiful friend, what happened to you? I wanted so much to help you but I had to just sit back and watch you destroy yourself until you called. I knew something was wrong. You never call me at 9 o'clock in the morning." I giggled through my sobbing and tears. Then this first angel of *The Magnificent Seven* stood up from the bed and sounded her trumpet. Hail and fire was about to strike. And so, it did.

"Brent, I need a witness lets go get this fucking junkie out of her house," Cindy said with vengeance in her voice, "I've been waiting to long for this. Party time is over for this asshole." Then Cindy turned to me, "You stay right here. Do not come over there cause I'm going to say and possibly do some things that aren't going to be too nice and I have my gun on me just in case."

"Ok. Good thing my dogs and cats are probably hiding underneath the bed!" I said in a sarcastic tone and a chuckle.

Cindy giggled, "Jeez! Even messed up, you're still a smart ass!" She gave me a wink and a smile as her and Brent headed out his front door to knock on my apartment door. The walls are very thin and I heard most of what went on. Cindy was right, it wasn't pretty. This was Cindy's recall of the event that saved my life on that dark dismal day. Andy swung open the door just as Cindy knocked, not knowing it would be her on the other side of the door.

"What do you want?", Andy said meanly.

She put the evilest smile on her face and walked in like she owned the place, and at that moment, she did. As she spoke very sternly and calmly to him she walked slowly with her finger pointed at him and pushed him with that slender finger as he walked backwards trying to avoid her. "Here's what's going to happen. You're going to collect your stuff and get the hell out of here right now. And I'm going to stay here and watch you collect your pathetic little things and once you leave you will never come back here again. Do you understand that? Or are you too fucked up to do it? Because I have no problem physically removing you."

"Wait a minute," Andy started, "This is my house now and we are going to just sit down and talk about this." He said taking a seat at my dining room table.

"Andy, let me let you in on my plan. If you don't start collecting your crap and leave, I am going to go out and buy you the best heroin money can buy and I'm going to buy a lot of it. Then I'm going to lay it out in front of you with a bag of needles and I'm going to watch your junkie ass do all of it because I know you won't be able to resist it. Then I'm going to wait until you pass out. It will be at that time I will put you in the trunk of my car and drive out deep into the Everglades and dump you where I know there is a swamp full of alligators. Am I making myself quite clear with you or are we going to sit here and talk about it some more?" She said cool as a cucumber.

Having heard this, Andy's reaction was priceless. It was then that he got up from the dining room table and grabbed his Rubbermaid tub and started packing his clothes and what little he had to his name into that tub and it literally took him six minutes to get out of my house. But as he walked out the door Cindy spoke up.

"Hold on junkie. You're not as dumb as you look and I'm smarter than you think. Give me the house key she gave you."

"Fuck!" Andy said turning around and handing Cindy the key. "Wait right there while I make sure it's the right key." Cindy checked the key against the lock and it was a match.

"Now go and don't ever let me see you here again."

***

With that, Andy left and started walking down the street with his Rubbermaid tub filled with his little treasures of his little life on his way to scope out his next victim . When Cindy and Brent came back over to get me, I was sitting there on the bed waiting for them like she asked me too. I couldn't wait to get back into my apartment. As I walked into my little home, there were my two little Chihuahua girls, Ginger and Simone. They slowly came out of my bedroom along with my two cats, Ace and Natasha. They peered around the corner into the living room and I dropped slowly to my knees on the floor in tears anticipating their timid walk over to me. As I looked at the four of them and realized how skinny they were my oldest little girl, Simone climbed up into my lap. I scooped her up into my arms and she lightly gave me a lick on my cheek as I held her so close to me not wanting to let go. My two baby girls were filthy. I couldn't remember when I bathed them last and they looked so hungry and tired. I packed some clothes and my two little dogs up and we went to Cindy's horse ranch. Brent took the key to my house as he was going to feed my cats and change the locks while I was gone and fix up the place a bit as Andy had broken the shower head too and well, the place was just disgusting. I was at Cindy's for four days and slept for two days. Ginger and Simone didn't leave my side the whole time. Cindy actually had to pick them up off the couch to eat. She said they wouldn't leave my side during my 2 day slumber.

Animals are spirit guides. I always looked at them as such. They love unconditionally and no matter what your sins are, they forgive you. Much in the same way as God does. It's no surprise that if you spell DOG backwards, it spells GOD. When I looked into their eyes that day that Cindy came and saved my life, I saw heartache, despair and hurt in them. The same way I felt and looked. They felt everything with me. Now when I look at them, they are fat and healthy. The fact that they didn't leave Cindy's couch for the two days I was passed out on it just goes to show you the loyalty an animal has for its owner. That's no accident. Just like God's love, it's there when you don't even deserve it. That kind of love can't be denied. That is true love and that is enough, because you are enough for them.

During those four days, Andy had stupidly left his Facebook messenger logged into my phone. I watched everything unfold. Including drug deals that were going down in Fort Myers, Port Charlotte, and Cape Coral, as well as with Matt and several of Matt's bandmates. I made sure I took screenshots of it all, in case one day he would try to harm me. But that would be a different chapter in a different story. I can't grasp the logic of doing drug deals on Facebook Messenger. Are people that messed up? I sat here shaking my head at the concept. Anyway, lets continue, shall we?

***

Now came the drying out stage, and what fun that was, not! A lot of sleep and a lot of eating. Cindy bathed my little girls and cleaned them up. They both ate a whole can of dog food every day for those four days. They slept and ate along with me as I entered into recovery, and they joined me with what dogs do best; unconditional love. It was the beginning of our new life. But I was still on the verge of losing everything. The struggle was real now. I couldn't cover it up with drugs and partying anymore. This was life in real time. I spoke with my real friends that were genuinely concerned. My boss that fired me three days before all this happened texted me as well. She was concerned for me as she knew exactly what was going on with me the whole time. She offered me my job back and I accepted. We agreed to give me two weeks so my bruised arms would heal as well as getting over the DT's. The clinical term for the DT's is *delirium tremens*. It's cause by the withdrawal of alcohol or drugs. Withdrawal from stimulants such as cocaine usually don't have any major-medical issues, however, when IV drug use is involved, it can lead to symptoms such as shaking, shivering, irregular heart rate, sweating and seizures that can occasionally result in death. After four days, the DT's started setting in and I was going home.

***

My friend Matt Vananyck stepped up to the plate with this one and didn't bat an eyelash when I called him. He'd read the post that Cindy put on my Facebook page stating that Andy had lied when he posted that I had a nervous breakdown. Everyone knew what I was doing and what had happened anyway so it wasn't a secret. Matt was right there for me. He is the third angel of The Magnificent Seven. He came and stayed the weekend with me at my apartment as I was not allowed to drive nor could I be alone since there was a good chance that Andy would show up. Matt hated Andy and the other Matt with every bone in his body. He and Cindy helped me clean up the apartment when we got there. Oh, my goodness, all the needles scattered about the house. So many were hidden as well. We threw out bags of needles, empty baggies of drugs, cocaine, heroin, pot, bowls, spoons, half empty water bottles. Everything in my house was disgusting. It was a reality check to say the least. I was sick and nauseous the whole time.

After Cindy left, Matt and I sat down to eat some dinner and watched a movie and talked heart to heart too. Matt, still to this day is a very close friend. He didn't have to stay with me and witness my downfall, help calm me through the DT's and help catch me, but he did. He still says to me, "Always remember Christina, I'm the good Matt." We dated briefly the previous year when me and the 'bad Matt' were on one of our multiple break-ups and just decided that we were better as friends. But when I cried out, he was there with the other six magnificent ones. Matt will always be my third angel. After Matt left I had to sit and think of what to do next. I had to tell Cheryl. But this was going to be the hardest thing that I would ever have to do. I would have to admit to my best friend that I needed help once again and that her best friend was a needle using addict. I sat for a week and contemplated it as I went through the most horrible DT's. Crawling around my floor in pain, trying to hold my head out of the toilet while throwing up nothing but stomach bile. I think at one point I had a seizure because I had blacked out and woke up on the floor and my tongue was in excruciating pain. I got up and crawled to the bathroom using the vanity to pull me up. As I looked in the mirror my mouth had blood all over it and my tongue looked like chopped up meat. I must have bit it somehow. As I looked in that mirror, I hated the woman that was staring back at me. How did I let this happen? How was I going to tell my best friend and her husband what happened? That on more than one occasion when we were hanging out, I was high as a kite and how I had become a mess from having a needle stuck in my arm. There was only one way to do it. Tell the truth. So I washed my mouth out with hydrogen peroxide and since I couldn't eat anything with a mangled tongue even if I was hungry enough, I went to bed. The darkness of my room was inviting with the sound of silence enveloping my mind. It was Friday night September 23rd and I had been going through the shakes and the shivers alone for a whole week. Now, in less than 12 hours my best friend in the world was going to be sitting in front of me and I would have to bare myself and tell the whole story.

I woke up Saturday morning and frantically started cleaning the house to make it look presentable for Cheryl and her husband Tony. I took a shower and put on some make-up. I was so pale and so skinny still. I looked like walking death and in thirty minutes they were going to be sitting in my living room. As I paced back and forth through my now beautiful, clean and OCD sanitized apartment, I was trying to figure out how I was going to do this without breaking down. Then, scaring me out of my converse sneakers, there was a knock at the door. I looked out kitchen window to make sure it was Cheryl and Tony and not Andy as I was experiencing severe paranoia at that point. I answered the door and welcomed my forth angel, my lifelong friend and her husband into my home offering them a drink. Of water that is.

We sat down on the couch, got comfy in the living room and then Cheryl spoke.

"Girl, what's going on? I figure it's pretty serious as this meet up is totally out of character for you."

"Well, I have to confess some things to you and Tony. Some things happened in the past year since getting out of the hospital from the hysterectomy and I want to come clean and tell you both. So, I'm going to take you through it and just let me finish before you say anything." I continued on, laying out the sordid details of the last nine months before Cheryl and Tony. From the initial onset of being prescribed the oxycodone and the morphine in the hospital, to Matt getting me the liquid heroin for the pain and to him and I starting to snort cocaine. I even told them about the one night all three of us were hanging out at the *Buddha* and how I was about to go onstage to sing with Matts band and I ran to the bathroom because I snorted so much coke that my nose started bleeding. I told them everything leading up to Andy shooting me up, and how I was now about to lose my apartment because I couldn't pay the rent. I told them about Andy stealing my car all the time and running through the toll booth without paying for it which had now resulted in

$1,100.00 in toll violations. I finally ended the traumatic story with me about to lose my license because of those toll fines. After I was done I was in tears. I admitted my fault in all of it and took the blame for the mistake I'd made. It was a lot for them to take in. Then Tony, with a deep breath said, "Thank the Lord you are alive. We are going to help you. You are not going to lose your apartment. Is there any way you can ask your sister for help?"

"Tony, I haven't talked to her in three years. During that time, I've been up here and haven't made the effort to contact her." After saying that I realized how much I missed my beautiful sister and my two gorgeous nieces. I pushed everyone I loved away from me because of the hurt and the pain. I didn't want to hurt anymore but I figured that it hurt more not having the people that truly loved me in my life. Cheryl, I assumed as the look on her face was pretty transparent, was beside herself. If I know my best friend the way I do, then I know what came out of her mouth was real. Because she already knew the answer.

"How do I help you stay clean? What do we need to do? I will do anything it takes to keep you clean." She had tears in her eyes. I mean after all; she was looking at a woman she never thought she would see. A broken-down shell of the strong woman I used to be.

"Cheryl," I said starting to cry even more, "You can't keep me stay clean. I must do that for myself. I must want that for myself more than anything in the world. I have to learn how to live my life again. But I can't do that if I lose everything."

"Then that's what we will do. We will make sure you have a roof over your head. We will make sure you don't lose your license. Now, what about your job?"

"They hired me back I start next Monday, and thank you so much! I will take care of all the other mess myself. I'll catch up on my car payment and I'll get the insurance on it." Uncontrollably, I started sobbing again. How could so many people love me so much after all the hurt and pain I put them through. Cindy, Brent, the good Matt, Cheryl, Tony and my family. How could they love me so much after all this? I didn't deserve them. They didn't deserve such a messed-up person in their lives. But they loved me. This whole time who I was, was enough for them. Now it was time to get life back on course and be enough for myself. I pissed Satan's messenger off by getting sober. But Satan wasn't done with me yet. He had a whole new plan. I went back to work and got everything in order. I was welcomed back with open arms. I caught up on my car payment and paid my insurance on my car. Cheryl and Tony helped me straighten the rent and the toll violations up. I started going to Narcotics Anonymous and I began to get back on track. Little by little I was fixing all the mess I had created.

I started reconnecting with a lot of people from my past. Two more high school friends from New York got a hold of me and even though we reconnected through social media a few years back, we spoke on the phone now almost every day. Celeste Mollica, my fifth angel of the seven and I were friends in High School and she was a beautiful girl back then. Now she was an outrageously gorgeous woman. She was model in New York with gorgeous dark brown eyes, long dark brown hair and a spit fire attitude. She was very versed in nutrition and health care so she immediately got a hold of me and we talked about my nutritional needs now that I was clean. I had to start building my immune system back up. When you are messed up like I was for any period in your life, your body goes through major trauma. It is filled with toxins that need to be detoxified from the body. But this needs to be done slowly. Just as you have messed your body up with drugs, your body can go into shock by detoxifying to fast. Even though I would've come up with a negative test for drugs, the havoc they expel in your body, immune system and organs is literally traumatizing for your overall health. Some people when they get clean, don't realize that in theory. One doesn't eat a whole heck of a lot of food while using drugs. So, they get clean and start eating like crazy, and usually not the best food for you. Truth of the matter is, you should ease yourself back into consuming food. If you go all out and start gorging food, you risk getting diabetes and other hematological issues. We all knew I had very low hemoglobin to begin with so the damage I did was immense. There was times that Andy shot me up and I didn't have enough blood to carry the drugs through my system so I had to massage my arms so the drugs could get through my veins.

Celeste developed a dietary plan for me all the way from Connecticut where she lives. She did a large amount of research on the foods to help me build a better body. I started back at the gym with light work outs. This especially helps with the DTs as sometimes the stress from the flashbacks can be intense and I would just get on the treadmill and run it out. Celeste had me on a strict vegetarian diet with little to no meat at all. We had to slowly build up my protein intake. My stomach wasn't used to eating healthy so the biggest thing that was happening was nausea. The reflux was killing me. I'd never felt heartburn and nausea at the same time but it was like throwing up in my mouth every time I ate. Even when I drank water I would get nauseous. I couldn't understand what was going on. I always felt like my head was three feet thick. I even felt high again sometimes. I chucked it up to eating food that my stomach wasn't used to.

I also told Celeste one night on the phone how I was feeling and she had her concerns about this.

"Something is wrong," she said. "You should be feeling better, not worse. Everything you are doing should be making you strong again not weaker."

"Celeste, I feel high all the time. Maybe it's just DTs or flashbacks. I know that can happen. But there is a lot of pain. My back is in excruciating pain. I don't have back problems. My skin is itchy all the time and I'm getting like a rash. I don't understand it. It almost feels like I'm allergic to something and I have the flu."

"Hum. I'm out of ideas. Let me do some research and ask the doctor I work for. Maybe he knows what those symptoms are and why you are just now experiencing them after 2 months clean."

With that we hung up the phone and as I went to sit on the couch from exhaustion, the whole room went into a tail spin. I was 63 days clean, but my body began shaking, I couldn't see straight and then my brain went foggy. I couldn't stand up because I was dizzy, the pain all over my body got so intense, my skin felt like it was crawling all over me. I could feel the blood flowing through my veins like I'd felt when shooting cocaine only two short months ago. I was alone in my apartment and terribly frightened. I went to get up off the couch and quickly fell to the floor in a fetal position screaming in pain but no one was there. The back and stomach pain was intense. I tried calling my friend Mary who lived down the street at the time but she said was too busy to come over. I later found out she was too busy moving Andy into her condo. That friendship ended because well, NA teaches us people, places and things. So, she was a people.

***

I needed someone who knew what they were talking about when it came to detoxing from drugs. The DTs were never this bad when my mom detoxed me 25 years prior. I never recalled feeling like I was spinning. I couldn't remember things. I trouble concentrating. It was almost like my brain didn't want to work. I called out to a few friends and ironically, Andy's old guitar player contacted me and immediately told me to get in the shower. Then put a large towel over my head and to sit under the flow of the shower with the water going as hot as I could take it. This is a technique used by a lot of people when they are going through withdrawals. It calms the senses down. Just for reference, if anyone is detoxing or has a friend or loved one who is detoxing, the *worst* thing you can do is to not be with them while going through an episode. It's the scariest thing to leave an addict going through withdraws alone. It feels like riding on a rollercoaster at the speed of light, while flying through a dark tunnel. For us, it seems there is no end. Especially when we start to hallucinate. Being alone is the scariest thing in the world to us. I started to hallucinate while I was sitting at the bottom of the shower. I remember it in my dreams sometimes. I saw Andy there, consoling me and then his face would turn into a hideously monstrous and evil shape ready to stab me with a needle. I would snap myself out of it screaming in the shower. The hallucinations were fierce. I thought to myself, how could I possibly be going through this after sixty-three days being clean? That was a bad withdrawal. Only, it wasn't a withdrawal at all. It was what was to become the biggest fight of my life.

***

I had a smaller episode of the same symptoms the next night and the following Monday early in the morning. I found myself sitting at the bottom of a hot as hell shower with a towel over my head at about 5:30

a.m. Not in all my life had I ever felt that much physical pain and now to compound it all, my mind was getting very foggy and my eyes felt like they had a film over them. I could see but it was more as if I was looking through a cloud. It's hard to explain how it felt. I was extremely exhausted and I couldn't think straight and I actually felt like I was high all the time again obviously without the use of drugs. I went to work that Monday morning on November 7, 2016 in a haze like state. I knew which way to go to get to work, but I don't remember actually driving there. It's like I went through the motions and was detached from myself the whole time while I was driving. When I got there, I went about my business as usual from what I remember. Then one of the installers said to me, "Christina, your eyes are yellow." I mentioned that I hadn't felt very well and went back to my office and got on Google. I started Googling all my symptoms. I was always one to self-diagnose to avoid having to go to the doctor and I was usually pretty good at it. As I typed in yellow eyes, brain fog, seeing cloudy, Google immediately took me to a website for symptoms of Acute Hepatitis C. *No!* This is not correct! It was about 11a.m. in the morning and this information had to be incorrect! I do not have Acute Hepatitis C! I read further the symptoms and the treatments and the eventual outcome. Also, the incubation period for Acute Hepatitis was twelve weeks to six months. It was the exact time frame of Andy shooting me up. If I did in fact have Acute Hepatitis C, Andy was the one that gave it to me. I was going to die and that was the last thing I remember. This is the account of how the story goes of what happen that day, as it was told later to me.

I walked out to the main office and started walking around in circles talking and screaming to myself. I didn't know where I was, what my name was, what year or date it was. I had no idea who the President of the

United States was and I didn't know my name. Bobby, one of the shop techs grabbed me and held me so I would stop walking in circles. The accountant had Bobby get in the back seat of her car with me as they rushed me to the hospital. When I came to, I was in the emergency room waiting to be seen. They took me down to get blood drawn. I hadn't had a needle in me for sixty-three days and they were about to hit the same vein as Andy did all the time. I grabbed onto the table as they put the tourniquet on my upper arm and I began to cry. Oh my God! The psychological torment I was enduring was enough to give someone heart failure. They had to take 6 vials of blood and as the needle went into my arm I held my breath and bit my bottom lip and just sobbed. Bobby stayed with me the whole time.

"Please hurry up! Please! Oh God, help me!". I was crying and yelling out to God to help me and I didn't even realize it.

"Christina, baby, go to your happy place! You're in your happy place. Nothing can hurt you there!", Bobby rushed over and knelt down in front of me and grabbed my free hand. "Look at me baby girl! Look into my eyes!" Bobby spoke to me with heartfelt sincerity. Little did I know that he was a needle user as well. He wasn't high that day thank God. I don't know if I would've made it without him. He spoke those words to me and had tears in his eyes as he was speaking very audibly and calmly this time.

"Go. To. Your. Happy. Place."

I felt a calm come over me as he spoke those words one more time to me. It was like I was back on the floor of my living room the day I overdosed when my father's spirit was holding me. I was again detaching myself from reality. The reality of someone sticking a needle in my arm. The reality of someone's dirty blood running through my veins. The reality of the grave mistake I once made that was now threatening my life more than I had ever imagined it would. I had received a death sentence from Satan's messenger. My friend Anne Marie Lago messaged me on Facebook to see if everything was alright as I had posted that I was being admitted into the hospital. I told her my symptoms and I also told her, I thought I had Acute Hepatitis C. She had been following my journey of sobriety and was concerned when she saw my post. Anne Marie and I were friends in New York in high school. She was a grade ahead of me so we weren't real close friends at the time but we shared a bond being of the Valhalla Viking Sisterhood. She was always kind to me and had been so proud of me for conquering my demons. We became very close friends in the months that followed. She was to become a very important part of my life as well as my sixth angel of *The Magnificent Seven*, never leaving my side for one moment and never doubting me or my journey. She was to become a pivotal asset to the journey my life was about to take and the adventure of a lifetime that was to follow.

Then I heard from another beautiful heart. Her name is Kimberly Bigelow. Kim is a beautiful girl with long blond hair, again with blue eyes and this charisma about her that lights up a room whenever she enters it. Kim and I had been friends for a few years and we always hung out together at the shows at the local R Bar. The last time she saw me, I was with Andy at the R Bar and I was high. Kim was concerned as well when she read my post due to the fact that she knew Andy and had a feeling that I might have relapsed. I told her as well what was going on. At this point the diagnosis wasn't in so I couldn't be sure what was wrong with me. But we all had our suspicions. Kim would later become another pivotal person in my journey and therefore, the seventh angel to sound the trumpets and to complete *The Magnificent Seven.*

The hospital started me on fluids right away as I was severely dehydrated. My liver enzymes had spiked so high that my liver was starting to fail. There was excruciating lower back pain and my brain felt like it was vibrating inside my skull. It was the most obscure feeling I had ever felt. Bobby went back to work as the hospital was now going to admit me for an indefinite stay there. My eyes were as yellow as caution tape now and my skin was yellow as well, almost green. My muscles and joints ached and I was so tired. But I had a lot to take care of. My little fur babies had no idea I wouldn't be coming home that night so I had to entrust them with someone that I knew would take care of them. I was about to call my first angel, Cindy and then just as that thought went into my head, my phone rang.

"Honey, what's going on? Are you ok?" It was Cindy reading my mind on the other end of the line. "No Cindy, I'm not. I'm in the hospital and they are keeping me here. My little girls are at home and I only trust you with them. I hate to ask you to help me again because you have done so much for me already."

"Stop it! I'm coming. Does Brent still have the key to your apartment?"

"Yes he does."

"Ok, I'm going to go get the girls and feed Natasha and Ace. I'll show Brent how you feed the cats now as well since your obsessed with keeping them as fat as sausages and I'll grab your toothbrush and pajamas and some essentials for you. I love you. I'm leaving Arcadia now. I'll be there soon."

"Ok. Thank you so much. Cindy, I'm sorry."

"I told you to stop that. I love you more."

"I'll call Brent and see where he is."

We hung up the phone and I called Brent. He was right near the hospital so he came over. Just as he got there, the next phlebotomist was walking in. Oh boy, did he come at the right time. Here they were again about to stick another needle in my arm. As the needle went into my arm the same horrifying episode occurred. I was hyperventilating this time and holding Brent's hand so tight. Crying and yelling at God again to help me. They took another six vials of blood not 4 hours later from the first one that afternoon. Throughout the next twenty-four hours I would have thirty-two vials of blood taken from me. That's enough needles to make a recovering addict go into mental shock. I gave my house key to Brent so he could give it to Cindy and keep his to feed my cats. Cindy went and got my girls and took care of them for me. She brought my essentials to me and stayed with me for a while. We talked a lot that night. Cindy was always matter a fact with me. Like I said, you don't call Cindy for a pep-talk. She's just not like that. You call her if you want a reality check. We talked about what my next option was.

"Cindy, if it is Hep C, there's other people that Andy was playing musical needles with. They need to know."

"Fuck them! I have no sympathy for them. They deserted you after you got clean and treated you like a door mat when you were fucked up. Let them deal with it themselves. You owe them nothing! Do you hear me? You. Owe. Them. Nothing!"

"But Cindy, they could die. They could be lying in a hospital bed as well fighting for their life. It's not fair that they should suffer because someone is getting their kicks dealing out a death sentence."

"Listen to me, you are not going to die. It will *eventually* kill you. I have no doubt it was Andy that gave it to you. There's no other way you could've gotten it. You just had yourself checked last May because Matt was cheating on you and your blood was clean. So, that only leaves one person, Andy. And if I see that mother-fucker, I will shoot him with no questions asked!"

I knew Cindy meant every word she said. If she swore to destroy you, you can bet on it that she would do everything in her power to do just that. Cheryl called as well while Cindy was there. She was going to bring me breakfast the next morning and be there when the doctor came in to talk to me. Cheryl has always been the one who advocates for me to the doctors. She is the only one who has access besides me to my medical records. I needed her to be there because now I had no idea what was going to happen. I was in a scary place and my brain was only half functioning because of the enzyme spike in my liver. Throughout the night I had two more sessions of blood drawn. Oh how psychologically messed up I was by this time as I also had a gastroenterologist come in that treated me like I was a low-life junkie, strapped me to the bed on my side and stuck something up my rectum for a culture that I never even till this day have I gotten the results from. I have no idea what test she did but I can tell you that being strapped to a hospital bed while they were pulling 6 vials of blood out of my hand now because the veins in my arms had collapsed on the last blood drawing session while some bitch doctor is sticking something up my rectum for a test that I knew nothing about is pretty fucking traumatic! They didn't even say goodnight to me. I just laid there crying helplessly in that hospital bed as they walked out and left me there with no hope.

CHAPTER 10

THE REDEMPTION

***

When the wicked advance against me to devour me, it is my foes who will stumble and fall. Though an army besiege me, my heart will not fear. ~ Psalm 27:2-3

When you decide to put your life out there for all the world to see and judge, you have to have faith that there's a God. The very thing that you thought would be the literal death of you, could very well be the one thing that gives life and your purpose. I was being used harder and with more condemnation than Andy, Matt or anybody could've ever used me before. You see, no one can use you as hard and with as much conviction as God does. Then, when he knows you've figured it out, the tests of your faith start entering the picture. In the words of C.S. Lewis, "Only a real risk tests the reality of a belief", and just like that, I was condemned by an army of fools.

It was 3'oclock in the morning lying in the hospital bed motionless, thinking about my whole life and the decisions I'd made from the beginning as a child until now. I asked myself what if I'd done things differently, would it have really mattered? What if I never left New York and Cheryl, or if I never sliced my wrists or if I never fell in love with Rob, would I be here right now? Further, what if I never married Brandon, or if my mom was here right now, or if I never married Larry and if my Dad was still alive, would I be here fighting for my life? What was the turning point? What got me here? Or was it the combination of a beautiful little girl who once held the world and all its possibilities in her hands who had just lost herself and who she was somewhere along the way. The hard truth of making desperate decisions in her life because all she ever wanted was to be loved unconditionally and whole heartedly. The plight and the search to be loved and to love in return had become an accumulation of desperate decision making that lead me to the death sentence I didn't ask for, nor did I deserve. Yet, it happened and as I laid there crying I felt a heavy weight on my soul. Not a weight that hurt, but a weight of a loving hand. Like something was touching my heart.

I'd never felt anything this warm inside me before. I suppose it felt somewhat like when I overdosed and felt safe when my father came to me. But it was much more than that. They say when you feel the Holy Spirit move through you it is a feeling like no other. I felt that spirit hold me that night. I hadn't spoken to God since the night my mother died and I cursed him in that Catholic Church. It had been twenty-four years since then. That's a long time to be running away from the one thing that will ultimately save you. That night I prayed for my soul like I'd never prayed before. I prayed for redemption.

"Dear God,

It's been a long since I felt you. I haven't been a good person at all. I cursed your name once and several times after that night when you took my mother. You took so much away from me and now you are about to take my life as well. Satan and his messenger got a hold of me and grabbed a hold of my life. I pray for you to save me. I lay down my life in your presence. You are my savior Jesus Christ. Please don't forsake me. I will accept your will. If I am to live I will glorify your name and if I am to die, then your will be done. But I will ask you "why" for many days. I have yet to be redeemed of my sins and I have yet to learn how to relive my life in your word. I can't change the past. But I can change the way I live the present and the future. Bestow on me your grace that I so don't deserve right now so that I may know you and your love for me. Heal me. I've got so much more left to do. Show me the path I need to take. And from this day forward let me walk in the light of your love for me. In Jesus' name, I pray. Amen"

***

Later that morning, another doctor came into the room and confirmed that I had Acute Hepatitis C. I took the news somewhat good considering I already knew in my heart that's what it was. Nothing can really prepare you for the notification of a death sentence. I was mad at myself for the mistake I made, I was mad at Andy for giving it to me, I was mad at Matt for bringing drugs into my life. But mostly, I accepted my part in all this. Yes, it was my mistake, but now I was thinking of all the other people who Andy may have infected. Just as I was thinking about that Anne Marie called me. I explained to her what was going on and she said, "Your voice should be heard for others that can't. I see you helping others in the future."

"I want to show the world what happened to me. What if he hurts someone else?" Little did I know the path that God had put me on was for a reason. There are *no* accidents in this life. Cheryl brought me breakfast that morning and showed up with her note book to be the diligent brain to my brawn as usual. As the doctors spoke, she took notes and ask the questions I couldn't. I had "brain fog" as they call it. It's when your enzymes spike in your liver, since it effects your neurological system it also effects your memory. I had short term memory loss because of the spike and it would months before I would ever be able to function mentally on a normal level. Brent came to pick me up at the hospital to take me home later on that day and I rested for the rest of the week and weekend to return to work on Monday. I had many conversations with my *"Magnificent 7"*. One of them was with Kimberly one night. It was Saturday, November 12, 2016, and Andy's band had a reunion show that night. I was still friends with the other guys in the band and I wasn't going to hurt that by coming out with anything. In fact, I wasn't exactly sure I wanted to say anything. This was definitely something I had to think about. I mean, people would hate me more than they already did. When you have so called *'friends'* who are easily manipulated by a false idol, they jump on the band wagon of false truths presented to them. No one was going to believe me and I would put my own name through the dirt. And for what? To warn people that didn't care whether I lived or died? For people that wouldn't lift a finger if I was on my death bed; which was exactly where I was headed.

"Christina, you have to tell people," Kimberly spoke with conviction in her voice. She's so passionate about the things she believes in and I always admired her for that.

"Kim, I can't. The reunion show is tonight and that will just make me look like I want to hurt Andy and the band. I don't want to hurt anyone anymore, but I don't want anyone else to get hurt.'

"Well, then I'm going to tell you something," she said starting with a deep sigh, "Andy was at a Halloween party that I was at a few weeks ago. He was throwing up blood all over the house we were at. There was throw up and blood all over. He threw up in the bathroom, on the floor, on their couch. And my friends that were having the party have 2 little girls. The oldest is seven years old."

I started to cry out, "No! No! No! Children? No! How could he do that? How can he put innocent children in danger like that? Oh my God!" I started pacing the floor in my apartment in disbelief, "Hurt me, ok I get it. But these are two little girls!"

Kim was now crying as well, "I know. I didn't want to say anything to you because you're health is fragile right now but please, can I please tell my friend and her family?"

"Oh my God, yes Kim! You have to! I can't stand by and watch people get hurt. Before someone else gets hurt, I have to say something."

We hung up the phone and was still pacing back and forth on my living room floor, sobbing and praying to God to hear me. I didn't want people to suffer because of my own ego and my silence to protect myself. It wasn't about me anymore. The path God was putting me on was not about me. It was about everyone else. I was to be His messenger to combat the evil that was creating a possible epidemic. That night I was bathed in the protective blood of Jesus Christ and the Armor of God was given to me to adorn my soul. Lord knows I needed it. For the war against Satan's messenger and my path to righteousness was at the very first stages. There was so much more to come.

***

Monday morning came and I called the people that needed to know I was putting it all out there on public social media. I spoke to Kim's friend Lisa, who Andy had put in danger about her family's role in this as far as her two little girls and husband were concerned. The lead singer of the band Andy was in and his wife were staying with Lisa. I gave Lisa permission to tell them who it was as they knew me very well. I got a phone call from them later on that morning.

"Hey, honey, it's Jeff and Tanya. You're on speaker phone, is that ok?"

"Yeah, that's cool. How are you guys? How was the reunion show?"

"It was really good. But I said to Tanya, Christina's not here. Something's wrong. I knew something was wrong." Jeff said sounding so solemn.

"Yeah, I really wanted to be there but I am so sick right now and I look sick. My eyes are as yellow as caution tape and if I was there, people would've known I was sick, so I didn't want to go. I didn't want to have to explain myself there. There's a proper time and place for things like that and it wasn't to be at your reunion show."

"Christina, I am so mad at Andy now. I never want to talk to him again. How can a person take somebody's life and do what he did to you consciously and deliberately?" Jeff was whole heartedly pissed off. "As of right now, I will never get on a stage with him ever again. I have nothing to say to him."

"Well, I'm sure Lisa told you what I'm going to do. I can't keep this quiet anymore. This isn't about me. I don't think it ever was. This is about protecting innocent people from getting hurt. I understand why he did it to me. But it was my mistake for allowing it to happen. Now, I need to turn my mistake into something that will help people."

"They are going to tear you apart Christina" Tanya said.

"I know they are and that's ok. I'm ready for it. If I tell my story and it saves one person from going through what I'm going through right now, then that is what it was all for.."

"I want to kill him right now. I want to murder him. I'm so pissed I can't even explain how I feel. We want you to know that we have your back 100%, and so does Lisa and her family." Jeff said with honesty and truth in his voice.

"I know. I thank you for that and your friendship. Now I have to go right my testimony. I'll let you know when it's posted."

"Ok. You're a strong woman Christina. We love you' Tanya said.

"I love you guys too."

With that, we hung up the phone and I began to write my testimony to be publicly displayed on Facebook.

With one very deep breath, and the hope that this reaches innocent people who deserve the truth, this is my story.

"It's been 63 days since injecting my last dose of illegal IV drugs, which over the previous 3 months before that, included cocaine, crack, oxy and dilauded. As most of you who have been reading my posts about my journey of sobriety it was sometimes great and sometimes horrific. But for the most part, I felt strong and healthy again. By shedding the toxic people from my life that I used to associate with, I felt all negativity and toxicity release from me. I made a conscious decision to put that treacherous traveled road behind me and thought that I had succeeded. Well, I was wrong. Two weeks ago on November 5th, some of you might have remembered I thought I was going through a bad withdrawal. I was hallucinating, my body and joints were in so much pain. I felt like my skin was crawling. My urine was dark like brownish red and that night left me absolutely

exhausted with the same thing happening again on Sunday night. I hadn't eaten for four days and the thought of food made me nauseated. Anything I tried to eat, I threw up and if I managed to keep food down, the reflux was disgusting. Remember all these symptoms because it wasn't a bad withdrawal.

Monday November 7th, I walked into work and one of the shop workers said to me, "Christina, your eyes are yellow!" I was jaundiced, along with abdominal pain and fever and still all the symptoms from the above paragraph. I started hallucinating at work later that morning and was rushed to the ER where I was admitted and thirty-two vials of blood samples were taken over the next twenty-four hours. That's pretty traumatic for an ex-junkie to deal with that many needles and the sight of the IV was making me want to vomit. While all that was going on, I had an ultra sound on my liver I was officially diagnosed with Acute Hepatitis C and in liver failure.

This is a direct result from sharing needles with Andrew. Yes, I was careless for my own regard as well as reckless, but the fact remains that there are many others that were too, but we own our mistakes, at least I do. I take responsibility for my actions and this admission is part of that responsibility. The problem now, is that Andrew has been notified by a very good friend of mine, this past Friday night. Andrew called me every name in the book and is trying to turn the tables around, in his fantastic way of manipulating people, when he knows that this did not originate from me. The fact remains that my last blood test was in March or April because some of you remember that a particular boyfriend cheated on me and I wanted to make sure he didn't give me anything, so I wasn't shooting up from that point.

The incubation period for Acute Hepatitis C is twelve weeks to six months before any symptoms show, or it can be detected in the blood. That incubation period also proves that Andrew is the one that gave it to me because that's when I started shooting up with him. There are other people he has and/or possibly has infected. I have been in touch with a few of them this morning. I made the decision to come out about this, not because I want attention and not because I wish to harm or defame anyone. The intention of this is to create awareness. Hiding what has happened to me and the actions that led up to it would be preferable to anyone in my position, but I could not, in good conscience, remain silent and watch others tumble into a similar fate. The most embarrassing thing is to go into a store and have to keep your sunglasses on because your eyes are as yellow as caution tape.

I came out about this mostly because there is an epidemic that is circling people that I care about, and people I don't even know. It's much larger and much more alarming than most of you probably realize. Some of them were stupid like me but owned their mistake and got tested. Some of them are infected because of other ways of contact. Because of his affiliation with certain people, this has the potential to effect so many in our circle of friends. Please, if any of you think you could possibly have it, please don't be embarrassed. Please help stop this now! If anyone has any questions you are free to contact me via private messenger, your secret is safe with me. I'm doing this because I don't want other innocent people to be hurt and have to go through the excruciating pain this disease is inflicting physically, emotionally and mentally on me. It's devastating.

If I can help save one person from this and help put a stop to him or anyone else carelessly or unknowingly spreading this to others, then my admission of this is what it was all for.

Namaste,

Christina

***

I can't tell you how many hate messages I got. From, 'You deserve everything you get.' to 'You're nothing but a loser junkie.' to 'If the disease doesn't kill you, I'll be happy to help put you out of your misery.' Funny thing is though, I had the *Armor of God* on my soul. There was nothing these people could hurt me with except words and really words were all they had.

You see, you can have proof for those type of people in black and white and they will still want to believe the lie because it's more exciting than the truth. I feel sorry for those people now. However, for peace of mind, I sought out to gather my own proof in black and white. Jason was always a good friend of mine. We had a fling a few years back right after my father passed away but that was about it. We always remained friends. He was a Lee County Sheriff's Office decorated Deputy and called me on occasion to check up on me after I had gotten clean. Not to mention that he is absolutely gorgeous, he's also one of the most honorable men I've ever met. I seem to always fluctuate towards the tall, dark hair, dark eyes kind of guys. I could call it stereo typing but, the dark hair, dark eyes guys never hurt me, it was always the blond guys with blue or hazel eyes. I'm going to have to make a mental note of that if I ever date again.

The night after I posted my admission testimony Jason called me to see if I was safe after I forwarded him all the threat messages I got along with all the drug deals that went down on Andy's Facebook messenger. When shit goes down, it's always good to have a cop friend to forward stuff to.

"Hey girl, it's Jason. Are you doing ok?"

"Hey hot stuff! Yeah, I'm ok. I just wish I could turn back time sometimes you know?"

"I know. But it just isn't that easy."

There was a moment of silence in me as a light bulb in my brain went on.

"Hey Jason, I have an idea. I need to ask you a favor. You can say no as it kind of goes against a work ethic for you."

"Oh Jeez, I'm afraid to hear what it is." Jason said with hesitation in his voice.

"Andy was in jail about 2 years ago for seven counts of grand theft and burglary. He did a bit of time and then got released to drug court."

"Oh, I don't like where this is going." He sounded worried and I giggled.

"I know he had to have his blood tested for hepatitis and HIV and a few other things when you are a felon and put into general population. Can you get me a copy of his test results from the jail? I need closure in black and white."

"Christina!" Jason retorted, "You know he was the one who gave it to you! Do you have any idea how much trouble I can get into if I get caught doing that?"

"Yes, I do. I'm sorry I asked. What am I thinking? Forget I said it. I'm thinking crazy."

"I'll come over after my shift tomorrow night. I'll print it out and bring it to you."

I was dumbfounded. Here I was again, not deserving of someone to put themselves on the line for me. But Jason was about to risk a lot. He was about to risk his world for me. A loser junkie like me did not deserve friends like this. Jason came over the next night like he promised. He came late in the night; he didn't want to be seen by anybody. I don't blame him on that. I mean, a cop being seen with a known recovering junkie wouldn't look too good in the eyes of the community. I got us each a cold bottle of water and we went to the couch and sat down.

"Well," I started, "what where you able to come up with?"

Jason reached into his coat pocket as it was a chilly winter night in Southwest Florida, and pulled out an envelope.

"Here," he said handing it to me, "Please Christina, please do not ever let anyone know it was me that gave this to you. When I read it, I wanted to throw my badge down and go hunting."

I slowly took the envelope from his hand and opened it. My heart started pumping so hard I could hear it thump in my head. As I unfolded the printed paper with the sheriff's emblem on the top I read Andy's full name and gazing down at all the tests that were done, my eyes fell upon the clinical letters HCV which stands for Hepatitis C Virus and next to those letters was the word *positive*. I started to get angry. I started to shake and all I could think of was this demon, this messenger of Satan purposely infected me. The rage that was burning inside of me was like none I had ever felt. Not even when Matt had cheated on me. I got up from the couch and started to walk away when I just fell to my knees and started screaming in the most agonizing voice.

"That mother fucker! Why! Why! Why would he do something like this!"

"Christina!" Jason came running over to me, "Baby girl, you have your closure! That's what you wanted!"

"Yes! But now you don't understand! He knew two years prior to infecting me! He knew! And I was just on the phone with David the other day and he said Andy was up in North Fort Myers shooting up with him and Andy was playing musical needles like it was a fucking game! Jason! He's hurting people and dealing out death sentences on purpose!"

"Jesus! Who's David?"

"David is a guy that used to come here, party, shoot up and get high. He saw my post about Andy infecting me and called me."

"Oh my God! Christina, you need a lawyer. He can be charged with attempted murder for this. It's more of an epidemic than HIV is right now, over 700,000 people die every year from it. Yes, you were the one that said shoot me up. But in a court of law, he's guilty for endangering your life and attempted murder because he knowingly shot you up with the same needle he used on himself."

"Jason, this isn't about me anymore. This is so much bigger than me and the worst thing about it is that it doesn't matter if I have this pathology report or anything. I have all the evidence right here in black and white, and still, no one will believe me. Not a single soul." I started crying for myself, my life but most of all, I started crying for all the people that Andy had potentially put in danger. My heart was breaking even more than it already was. My soul hurt so much for these people that I didn't know and that I may never meet. My head was spinning and I was having trouble talking. The enzymes in my liver were spiking again and effecting my thought process.

"Christina, listen to me," Jason said grabbed my shoulders to try and calm me down, "Getting this upset isn't good for your health right now. You have to concentrate on you. You have to fight for you. Not everybody else. Fuck them! They don't give a rat's ass about whether you live or die. And right now, you have to live! You have to get cured!"

"Jason, that treatment is $120,000.00! There's no way I'm going to get that treatment. I'm going to die because of this! Andy delivered me a death sentence and in turn he's going to be the one that kills me! This is my fate. This was destiny. To lose everything I ever loved and to die alone. I guess I sort of deserved it."

"No, you don't. Yeah, you can be crazy. But you don't deserve to die."

Jason stayed with me for a few hours. He made me something to eat and some hot lemon tea with turmeric to calm my liver. We watched a movie and I suppose he stayed until I fell asleep and he put me to bed. I woke the next morning feeling lost. I had to do something, I just didn't know what. I'd been keeping a journal of my journey from the first week I got back from Cindy's house when she had saved me up until now. I felt the hand of God on me again like I felt in the hospital. I felt compelled to write. And I wrote it all down. I wrote everything down, the good, the bad and the unknown.

***

The next day at work, Anne Marie, Kimberly and I were talking in our online chatroom about what my next step would be. My head had been spinning and I couldn't remember things so I had to constantly write everything down. Kim was battling the pharmaceutical companies for me while Anne Marie was trying to keep my crazy side on the down low. She was reaching out to our high school friends from New York that could possibly have some resources for me. Celeste was in her own battle with the hospitals and the doctors trying to get me treatment. She even went all the way to the State Representatives to *The Center for Disease Control,* trying to help get some answers as well. So many people where giving their time to help me when I couldn't help myself. I still needed a bunch of blood tests done and the thought of having another needle stuck in my arm was to devastating to think about. On the way home that night I cried. I cried hard.

Sobbing for myself; the pity party was big. I had put enough stress on my *Magnificent 7*. I didn't want to call any of them. I'd put them through enough. I thought about the fact that I knew exactly how much I needed to shoot myself up with to kill myself. I had made my mind up, I was giving up. Kim had started a *Go Fund Me* account for my medical treatment which yielded a nice sum to pay for my first doctor visit, and to get the ball rolling on my blood work. But there wasn't a hope in me anymore. I had no fight left. I was so tired and so sad. I didn't want the charity. I know in her heart and Anne Marie's heart, that they wanted to do anything they could to help me get the treatment to cure me, but in reality, no one should've ever had to pay for my mistake. I actually felt horrible about having that funding. I was better dead in my eyes then to have innocent people that I didn't deserve to help me. I did this to myself. I held the gun, and Andy pulled the trigger. I picked up my phone and started to scroll through my contacts looking for Andy's drug dealer that I had become friends with for a while. I hadn't talked to any of those people since I had gotten clean so when he heard my voice he was happy.

"Hey girl! Where's my favorite been hiding?"

"I've been in recovery."

"Ah! You need to break out a bad habit?"

Then I got another call, I looked at my phone and it was Cheryl.

"Let me call you back."

I switch over to Cheryl's call.

"Hey Cher, what's up?

"Nothing, I was just thinking of you and wanted to call. How are you holding up?"

"Ok, I guess." I said quietly.

"Yeah? Sure, doesn't sound like it." Jeez, she knew me better than I knew myself sometimes. Then I let it out. I let it all go.

"Cheryl," I started crying again, "Why me? Why me Cheryl? I know I hurt a lot of people and I probably deserve some sort of punishment. But a death sentence? Cheryl it's not fair. I worked so hard to stay sober and clean and I fixed my fuck ups. It's not fair! It's not fair!"

Cheryl spoke in a loud tone of voice I had never heard from her before. "Ya know what? You are right! It's not fair! But you are the strongest bitch I know! You have had some lousy hands handed to you over the years and lost so much and every time you have ever fallen I have always been a witness to you getting back up and dusting yourself off. You always get up and head right back into the fight of your life. You have always fought back! No matter what happens to you, you always have gotten back up and conquered your down fall. I wish I was like that! I wish I had the fight in me that you have always had. And again, you're right! It's not fair! But God never puts on you more than you can handle and by God Christina, He thinks you are one bad ass bitch! Now, are you going to sit and cry about it or are you going to be that strong woman who I call my best friend and write that book I've been telling you to write for the last decade?"

There was a beautiful silence on the phone for a moment while I took in everything Cheryl had just said to me.

"Do you know how unbelievably humbled I am right now. For you to say what you just said to me and mean it. I always thought I failed you as a friend and here you are telling me that God thinks I'm a bad ass bitch." We both laughed and cried I think. "Cheryl, what if it was someone else that got infected and wasn't emotionally or mentally able to handle it? I suppose it happened to me for a reason."

"That, my friend is why you need to write your memoir. Your story is one of loss and despair. But there are beautiful moments as well. You are and always have been a survivor. You can help people Christina. Before it's too late for them or while they go through it. You can be their inspiration. You are about to go through the fight of your life and I know you, you will not fail."

I never called Andy's drug dealer back. I got home that night, dusted off my computer and began to write. I wrote it all down and during the process, I healed. So many things, situations and issues came back to me. There were times that I experienced severe panic attacks while trying to write certain experiences. I would recreate the scenes in certain rooms of my apartment to remember what it felt like to actually be there again. I would revert to the mindset I had and slip silently with my computer into the darkness again. But the reckless love of God stood by me and when that chapter would be finished He would pull me out and give me the strength to continue on to the next chapter. I became a hermit not wanting to walk outside into the world except for work, church, the grocery store and NA meetings. I found serenity in writing and hobbies. One in particular was Bible Journaling. Bible Journaling is the art of getting closer to God through creating artwork over the scriptures in the Bible. Some see it as a sin to cover Gods words with paint and embellishments but to me it is a form of communication and a sort of scrapbooking my feelings towards God. It's one of the ways I stay connected to Him. Every day through writing and my Bible Journaling, I was creating an intense relationship with God. But, I found myself slipping away from the human race. I was scared of people now. I was scared of being hurt and I was scared of losing myself again. Addiction is a force to be reckoned with. It is very easy to slip back and honestly, if I did I would've died. The damage I did to my body during that time was so severe that I do believe if I had ever slipped, I wasn't going to come back. That scared the hell out of me. I was now racing against borrowed time and there was no room or time left to mess up. The evil forces of Satan kept working on me and as each one arose, I conquered every one of them. While I rose to the occasion of a beautiful life, I watched all of Satan's messengers fall. That was the grace of God working to protect me and I made it out of that dark dismal abyss alive.

CHAPTER 11

FORGIVENESS

***

But I say to you, love your enemies and pray for those who spitefully use you and persecute you. ~ Matthew 5:44

You would think people would want to see someone overcome insurmountable odds. Unfortunately, the norms of society will show you how evil and wicked people are. The human race brainwashes us to down grade those who have fallen, it's in our nature to do so. We are a vain society that puts more emphasis on what our neighbor has and then once they fall, it's an "I told you so" festival or we do everything we can to keep that person down just so we can shine. The truth is, the reason we are doing harm to others is because somewhere in our subliminal consciousness we are scared or feel unworthy ourselves so we continue to lie about our own achievements just to look better in other people's eyes. You see, the only approval you will ever need is Gods approval. I realized this when I started writing this book. I was always looking for the praise and approval of other people that shouldn't have held any significance in my life. I wasn't good enough for them, I would never be good enough for them. But, I started to realize I was good enough for God and that was all that mattered.

With my drastic change in diet and my dismissal of the people, places and things that got me there in the first place I started to feel my self-worth come back. Little by little, one day at a time, my life started blooming like a rose that had suddenly come back to life. I was slowly becoming the woman God intended me to be. Every day yielded a new amazing outcome. But the loneliness I felt? Oh my God, the loneliness would break me down daily.

***

Thanksgiving came and went and Christmas was right around the corner. Even though publicly I portrayed myself as this warrior of addiction, my realization of the loneliness I felt was intense. I would spend Christmas alone that year as I had multiple times in the past but that year was different. The void left in my heart was a pain I felt through my very soul. I decided it was a good time to start deep cleaning my apartment. I had done everything to turn that apartment around into looking nothing like it did a few months ago. It became my sanctuary again and I became obsessed with it and God. I would recite scripture while cleaning. The relationship I had with God was growing and through writing about my journey I got closer and closer to Him. I had tried living my life my way and well, the outcome was obviously not so great. God was the only thing I had to hold onto. He was the only one there when I would cry out to Heaven. He always had the most amazing signs he would give me.

"Lord, please show me a sign that I'm not alone. This is killing me. I am a diseased and worthless woman and you stood by me all these years waiting for me to be still and turn around. That's all I had to do. I did it and now what. Now what do I do?" I was praying while mopping my floor and trying to figure out what this thing called life was all about. I prayed all the time and for everything. It didn't matter where I was or what I was doing, I prayed. I had to learn everything over again. I had to learn how to pay bills. I had to learn how to do laundry. I had to relearn structure and stability. Heck, I even had to learn how to grocery shop again. It was confusing to me because I finally came to Jesus and even though I knew I wasn't alone in the world and in a dark place, it just felt like I wasn't completely out of the rabbit hole. There was something always missing. Some void that was there. I learned that no one can fill a void, only God can. I started reading a devotional every morning and every night. My relationship with God became so intense. I filled up every moment of my days and nights with God and scriptures. At times I felt like I was being a little bit to forward with my friends on the whole 'God is great' concept of living and I would get very upset now when they used the 'God dammit' phrase in front of me. My whole concept of living changed right down to the way I spoke. There were no more severe cuss words that came out of my mouth and I sure as anything didn't use the 'GD' or 'JC' phrase anymore. In fact when people would say it, it would make me cringe.

Christmas morning, I started to think about the last Christmas present my father bought me in 2011 before he died that next March. Oh, how I would love to have my beautiful flute back. Andy had pawned it for drugs and when I found it missing after I got back from Cindy's house when I got clean, it broke my heart to find that it was gone. I searched all the pawn shops in Fort Myers and Cape Coral and actually found it. It was a limited addition Geimenhardt made in Germany and it was sterling silver. My father paid thousands of dollars for it. I found it in a pawn shop at the foot of the Cape Coral bridge. They had it on the shelf for $6,500.00. I left the pawn shop that day and threw up in the parking lot. The last beautiful memory I had of my father had been taken from me and had given Andy and whoever was with him at the time an incredible amount of cocaine. As I continued that morning cleaning my house completely enraged with a broom in my hand as I remembered that trip to the pawn shop, I stopped praying and started screaming in my apartment. My poor little Chihuahuas must have thought I was absolutely nuts. I started cursing Andy for taking everything from me. I cursed myself for allowing it to happen to me. I went in my bedroom and tore everything apart looking for everything. My parent's jewelry was gone. My cameras were gone. Every single piece of musical equipment I owned was gone. I screamed and screamed. On Christmas day 2016 I spent it cleaning my house, praying and screaming. Then it got quiet and like a zombie I walked out my front door with my broom in hand to sweep the porch. As I opened the door and turned around to start sweeping, there on the table near the door, laying in its case of indigo blue velvet, shining in all its silvery beautiful brilliance was my flute. The last gift my father had given me before he died. Resting up against the open case was a Christmas card. The only words on the card were:

Merry Christmas Christina

Enjoy Your Journey

***

My flute had been returned and by whom I have no idea and I still don't know. What an unbelievably generous thing to do. The few people I've told didn't have that kind of money to purchase back from the pawn shop. I remember staring at it months prior and tears welling up in my eyes then down my face. The pawn shop owner was an old man that I had told my story to but even though I had pawned things there before, I doubt he would've remembered me. Or did he?

"Can I help you?" he asked.

"No. There's nothing and no one that can help me." I said as tears started to creep out of my eyes. "I'm just admiring the last gift my father gave me before he died. I came home from rehab and noticed it was missing and I finally found it. It's right there on your shelf."

"Are you going to be ok? I'm so sorry. If I could give it back to you I would." He said with a tremble in his voice. I actually thought he might care. Imagine that, an old man that didn't even know me might care for a junkie like me.

"It's ok," I said as the tears were now streaming like a flood stinging my cheeks. I started to get nauseous, "It's not your fault I trusted the wrong people in my home and my life. People that took advantage of me while I was too blind and too stupid to see it happening. I deserve everything I get and everything that is taken away from me. Including having the one thing that meant everything to me to be taken away and sold for a fix. You're a business man and I understand that." I turned around sobbing and headed to the door. I stopped for a second to look back at my beautiful flute. With a sickening feeling in my gut I thought I would never see it again as I turned around and continued out the door in a nick of time only to get violently ill in the parking lot. After I finished vomiting by the side of my car I jumped in my little SUV and turned the key in the ignition. I looked up and the old man was at the door looking out the window at me with a painful hurt in his eyes. It would be the last time I ever stepped foot in that pawn shop.

***

As I looked at my flute sitting on the table outside my door that Christmas morning I immediately thought of the old man. Could he have remembered me and looked my address up? I suppose he could have but how unlikely would that be? I started sobbing with my head in my hands knowing I had asked the Lord for a sign and he gave it to me. He was with me and knew my heart ache of feeling alone and then presented me with the biggest memory of my father. I knew I would never be alone. I knew that I had now taken refuge under the wing of God. I knew that I would be able to fight the battle of my disease that was in front of me and I knew He was always with me no matter what. As I ran my fingers over the flute a calmness took hold of me and somehow, some way I knew everything, eventually was going to be exactly the way it was supposed to be. It was all according to His will. He saw me in the darkness and showed me the light. It was just a slight speck of light but if I followed it and took that step of faith through the door of hope that lead to His unconditional love on the other side, the blessings and miracles that He was about to bestow on me would be the greatest journey I would ever walk. I was ready for another adventure. This time my adventure would be with the Holy Spirit.

The miracles didn't end with my flute being returned to me. My juicer blew up one night and I posted the picture of the poor piece of kitchen equipment and a random person in Minnesota saw the post. At this point juicing my food was the only way I could eat. My liver wouldn't process food any other way. Well, 2 weeks later, the crème de la crème of digital juicers showed up on my front porch. Those things are expensive! I was resulted to a most humbling state of mind as I opened the box to find other articles of inspiration including a beautiful wooden statue of an angel. Three weeks after that, a huge box showed up on the front porch as well. As I opened it, the box presented to me my two violins that Andy had pawned as well. A friend of mine decided to go investigating and found one of them in the United Kingdom. He purchased both violins back and sent them to me. These are miracles. The likelihood of these things happening to a person is rare. These miracles brought me to my knees praising God and the people who stepped forward to see these miracles through. I prayed to God every day for blessings to be bestowed on each person who saw it in their heart to present me with these gifts. This was grace at work. Whether it was the old man at the pawn shop or some random person that followed my public journey of salvation on Facebook. It did matter who it was but I wanted that person to be blessed for the rest of their life here on earth. They sure as heck deserved it. I prayed for a lot of people during that transition time.

As I frequented the Narcotics Anonymous rooms and started going to church on a daily basis, praying for people and forgiving people became easier. But the nightmares continued. I was past my 90 days clean date and then the rollercoaster commenced. I wasn't scared of anything. I felt like I had this shield around me and a protector at my side by day. But at night the nightmares haunted me. The Hepatitis was working on my body and my brain. I would be fine during the day but at night I was afraid to sleep. I had already had a rock thrown through my window by someone who evidently didn't like the fact that I was publicly displaying my journey of sobriety and that fear just added to the grotesque images I would see when I finally did sleep. I would dream of Andy sticking me with thousands of needles in my arms and feet like some crazy Freddy Kruger Horror flick and wake up in a panic attack too scared to go back to sleep. The night sweats that the Hepatitis produced were excruciating as well. My body temperature would skyrocket and I would rip my bed clothes off just to have my temperature drop so drastically to the point I was shivering and frozen. Through this I kept my faith in the Lord. He was going to get me through this.

***

I finally decided on two things; I needed health insurance and I needed to find my parents jewelry. One of the nightmares I had was sadistic. Andy would be stabbing me with needles while I was bound and tied up all the while dangling my parents' jewelry in front of me. It was just another item of sentimental value that he had stolen from me and that I stupidly let happen. I had a feeling I knew who had the jewelry and I was right. I messaged his other drug dealer and yeah, he had a few of them. Jay was one of those dealers that despite what he did for a living, he had somewhat of a conscience. Andy had always used my phone so I knew what number was Jay's. I texted him one afternoon and much to my surprise he texted back and then I called him. I describe the jewelry to him and sure enough he had it. But there was a catch. He had given Andy $280.00 for my parents' college fraternity and sorority pins and necklace, my father's onyx ring and my mother's first engagement ring so, I had to buy it all back.

"I'll pay you the $280.00 if you can give me a couple of weeks. I can't pay it all off at once but I can pay half this week and half next week" I said pleading him to work with me.

"Ya know, I had a feeling this was stolen. It looked to sentimental to be given to him. He's an asshole and I will never sell him anything ever again. I'm done with him. Yes, of course you can pay it off." Jay said totally disgusted at Andy.

"Oh, thank you so much." I said gratefully.

"No worries my friend. And for the record, I'm proud of you getting clean." he said in a brotherly tone of voice. Wow! Imagine that, a drug dealer who cares. Go figure.

Two weeks later after paying Jay $280.00 to pay off Andy's fix from over 3 months ago, I had my parents' jewelry in my hands. My mom's necklace was all knotted up and I remember sitting in the parking lot in my car where I met Jay for my final payment to him, looking at and untangling her necklace. A serenity came over me and once again I felt the hand of God on my heart. As I untangled the necklace I felt as though my life was untangling in my hands. As I sobbed trying desperately to untangle the necklace, I came to the last knot and as it unfolded before me so did my life and my forgiveness for Andy. I never forgave him and that is what was holding me back from my next step in this journey. He had crucified me publicly and the awful things he said while I was not being that far into my recovery, almost lead me to relapse. I had in that instance, forgave him for every transgression he committed towards me. I forgave him for stealing my beautiful flute and violins. I forgave him for stealing my beloved parents' jewelry. I forgave him for knowingly giving me the death sentence I now carried in my blood. I forgave Andy at that perfect moment for everything. But I didn't forgive him for him, I forgave him for me. I let go of so much hate and so much anger that day. I forgave Rob for shooting himself in the head. I forgave my mother for letting my dad slam my head into the ground. I forgave my dad for doing it. I forgave Brandon for not staying married to me. I forgave Larry for beating me senseless. I forgave my sister for not talking to me for 3 years and still not since I got sick. I

forgave my grandmother for disowning me and my sister. I forgave her when she told me that it made her sick to her stomach look at me because I looked just like her dead daughter who just happened to be my mother. I forgave Matt for constantly cheating on me. I forgave all the people who took advantage of me when I had money and drugs just to turn around and leave me when I became a junkie, went broke and got sick. I even forgave the friends and people that knew or had an inkling of the truth that I speak and didn't stick up for me. But I didn't forgive all of them for them. I forgave them all for me. I couldn't hold on to that anger anymore. That day, I let all of it go and from that day forward I always kept Andy in my prayers.

CHAPTER 12

GOD'S NOT DEAD

***

Then Simon Peter answered Him, "Lord, to whom shall we go? For you have the words of eternal life. ~ John 6:68

When you are still, you finally realize that all the trials of life aren't just trials. They are stepping stones and the way God invokes knowledge into us. Sometimes I just want to slap, shake the crap out of people and yell at them. I want to say, "Look! Look what He has done in my life! You can have all of this serenity too if you just believe and find your faith!" But sadly, the truth is, you can lead a horse to water but you can't make them drink. I was once that person, but when my way failed, there was only one way I could go and that was God's way.

***

We were a few months into the New Year of 2017 and things were looking up. I acquired health insurance and finally got all the blood testing done that I needed. God bless Cheryl for going with me and holding my hand through all those doctor appointments. Every time they would stick me with a needle to draw blood I became this shaking and convulsing mess of an ex-junkie. She would turn my head away from the puncture site and hold on to me as I shook and cried. I can't imagine what she felt inside while trying to keep me calm. I was starting to get a whole new perspective on life. It was a grand feeling to be sober and have the incredible support system. I knew *The Magnificent 7* were cheering me on and as each snippet for every chapter of the book got posted, I knew I was doing what God had called me to do. My Infectious Disease Specialist, Doctor Ramirez was amazing. He treated me like a human being. Not like that last doctor in the hospital. My genotype for Hepatitis C came back as genotype 1A. That was the most curable form of the disease. My viral load went down considerably within 12 weeks. I was experiencing what doctors call *'spontaneous emission.'*

"Christina, I've got some great news for you. Your viral load was 4 million when you were in the hospital and now it's down to 1,136. But, I have to say it's quite baffling too me though."

At my surprise of the good news I couldn't understand why he said that. "In a good or bad way?", I said hesitantly.

"Well, you have ITP as you know so you are the least likely candidate to experience such a drastic viral load drop. You consequently, because of your anemia, don't have enough good blood to fight off and keep the Hepatitis at bay. So, I'm not sure what is going on, but your body is fighting the infection when the odds of you being able to do that don't exist." Dr. Ramirez said.

ITP is short for Idiopathic Thrombocytopenic Pupera. It only happens in AB+ or AB- blood and I have AB- blood. It's the most uncommon blood. It's a Rh-negative factor blood type which some people believe to be descendant of fallen angels or more hysterically enough, aliens. ITP is handed down genetically from mother to child. My mother was diagnosed with it at the age of forty and five years later she was dead from cancer. ITP is simply low levels of blood platelets that prevent bleeding. It usually combines itself with the diagnosis of anemia and one needs to take extra precaution when exerting some regular activities and to avoid getting cut or an open wound due to the fact that to stop bleeding is a very difficult task. It is quite a rare blood disorder as there are fewer than 200,00 cases a year but is treatable not curable.

The joy and peace that came over me as Dr. Ramirez spoke was entirely overwhelming in a very good way. As I sat there in his office with my case worker, I thought about the absolute irony of it all. My eyes got big and a gasp came out of me as I bowed my head and said, "I know why. It's because God's not dead."

Dr. Ramirez looked at me and studied me for a second and then with a huge smile on his face he responded, "No, He surely is not Christina. He is surely alive."

"Doc, I prayed and prayed for redemption and gave my will up totally to Him. This is His response. There's no other explanation for it. You're telling me that it's clinically impossible for my body to be fighting off this disease the way it is because I essentially don't have enough 'good blood' to do it, yet it's happening. There's only one answer to that."

"Well my dear, whatever it is that you are doing, keep it up. Because essentially, it's going to save your life. If you don't get treatment you most likely have about a year left. You see, even though you are having *'spontaneous emission'*, the damage to your liver is severe enough that if your liver fails again, you're not going to make it."

"I'm prepared. Let's get me some treatment." I said like the true warrior of Christ I had become and with that, I left with the prescription for Harvoni in my hand. I had the golden ticket!

Harvoni is the break through drug cure for Hepatitis C infection. It is very hard to acquire and very expensive. A twelve - week treatment is approximately $120,000.00, and here I was holding the golden ticket in my hand as I had to make sure the insurance would cover it. The only problem was, I didn't know the government wanted you on your death bed fighting for your life before they would even consider possibly granting you authorization for it to be administered. So just like that, I was denied treatment. The research I did showed that 99% of the time, the new Obama Care policies will not authorize treatment until you are in stage 4 liver cancer or have stage 4 cirrhosis of the liver. Then by that time, treatment is useless because you're going to die from the cancer or cirrhosis anyway. That's the way they get out of having to pay for the treatment even though you pay a higher premium to carry that coverage. You have to have an amazing doctor that is willing to go to bat for you and well, that's usually hard to come by because honestly, when you're an ex-junkie, they always take relapse into consideration. Dr. Ramirez was one of those doctors that believed in me. He never gave up even when I did. I got denied a second time and then a third time. Well, I knew another that was denied three times. And though I would never put myself on the same righteousness scale as Jesus, I kept thinking He got denied three times by the disciple

Peter and look what happened. Jesus was brought into eternal glory. So at the third denial of my treatment it was time to break some news to my sister. I decided to make that dreaded phone call. The one that no family member wants to hear.

"Hey, sissy what's up? How are you feeling?" D.D. answered with hope in her voice. We rekindled our relationship as sisters a few weeks prior and that tumultuous and turbulent time when I had held so many grudges against her. It was never really her fault. It was both of ours. It was the sibling rivalry I had engaged in and not feeling like I was enough while all the good things in life fell perfectly into place for her. Now I had a different outlook on all that. I was happy for her. While I had made a complete debauchery of my previous life, she watched as I fell and realized she needed to take a completely different path in life and avoid the complications that my life presented. But when we talked that night, something happened. She revealed how she really felt. Something she had never done before.

"I'm ok. Tired and nauseous but for the most part, hanging in there." I answered trying to match her tone.

"We've been sisters for way to long. What's up? I can tell something isn't right." She said as concern was the trade off in her voice.

"We need to talk about something very important. Now hear me out before you respond," the phone was the sound of darkened silence, "I've been denied treatment and the prognosis is not good. I may have a year left and I need your help to put everything in order. I don't want to leave things the way Dad did. I don't want to leave a mess for you to clean up."

"No! I'm not doing it!" D.D. yelled into the phone, "I'm not giving up on you! I lost Mom and Dad! I am not going to lose you too! I won't let this happen and I am refusing to believe it or give in. That's Satan trying to trash our hope and I will not let him do that! Not to you and not to everyone who loves you!"

"D.D. we have to be realistic about this. It's not a fairy tale. This is real life. I'm not going to make it and I need you to be that strong, kick ass sister that I taught you how to be!" I contorted back at her.

"Christina, I was never strong, never kick ass. You were always the strong one for me when I hid my head in the sand every time I wasn't able to handle things and situations. I hide from issues. You are the one that always fights. I'm not about to switch roles with you now. Don't you dare give up on me!"

All of a sudden, we both started crying. As I felt defeated, D.D. rose up with strength in her that I had never experienced in the forty-two years we had been sisters. She became that sister that I had taught her to be and she didn't even know it. She took one from my book and my life. All those years she was meek and just turned her back on issues with my crazy life, she finally stood up to the occasion. Through my tears a chuckle came into my voice.

"So much for not being that strong, kick ass sister huh?" we both smiled through a flood of tears, "You have to promise me that Ginger, Simone, Natasha and Ace will not go to the shelter. Promise me my fur-babies will be safe after I'm gone. Don't let anyone take them. Ginger and Simone are to go to Denise or Cindy and Natasha and Ace are to go to Cheryl. Everything else you can sell. I don't care about the material things. But the fur-babies, promise me you will take care of them and see that they get to right places and the right people."

"Oh Christina," as she started to talk I knew she was crying, "I promise. I promise they will be safe. I love you so much sissy."

"I love you too sissy. To the moon and back I will always love you first. I'll talk to you soon."

We hung up the phone and I broke down in tears. Every emotion and every feeling came out of me. I was sad, I was happy, I was hurt, I was scared, I was mad and I was grateful. I was grateful and thankful for everything. The good and the bad had balanced out and I was content in knowing that there was another adventure that was awaiting me on the other side. That was faith in knowing that there is a God. In that moment, I wasn't afraid to die. I had accepted my fate and now as I sat on my back porch and thought about my whole life and the regrets I could possibly have, I couldn't think of any. I was serene in the fact that He made everything work for my good. God was there the whole time. For twenty-five years I had rejected Him and painted Him to be a really good magician who wrote a fantastic fairytale. I ran away from Him like the speed of light, but He had been chasing me the whole time. All I had to do was stop, be still and turn around. He took that journey with me through life straight down the darkened rabbit hole and rejoiced when I came out of it. I may not have made the right choices in life, but for right now, for whatever time I had left, I was going to make it all count. I was determined to make it all right.

***

After the emotional call with my sister, I had to pull myself together. I mean after all, I had a book to finish before I was too sick to type and I had friends I had to call and break the news to. *The Magnificent 7* was the first phone calls I made. Those were hard enough as I still had Lisa, my editor as well to call. I had to make sure that this book would be finished and published in the event that I wasn't around to see it happen. But, the one phone call above all phone calls that needed to be made was to Heather. Heather was the first person I met at my new church, Cape Christian. Her and I had talked on occasion and she knew my history of drug use and she was always praying for me. I felt connected to her and she was a good friend and still is to this day. She worked at the church and was there the first day I attended service and we became instant friends. Sometimes you just know in your heart who your tribe is and she would play a pivotal part in my recovery as well. She is my spiritual warrior friend. When things get a little crazy, I always call or text Heather. She is always ready with prayer for me.

"Hey girl, how's it going?" she answered in her always upbeat way.

"Meh, I'm ok. Sorry I'm calling late but I have something hanging on my heart and I need a favor." I said timidly for what I was about ask would be a big decision I was making in my life.

"Sure, name it!"

"Well, I've been denied treatment for the third time. It doesn't look to hopeful and before I am too sick to do it, I want to be baptized. Can you help me set that up?"

"What do mean? Before you're too sick? Oh my God! Are you serious? What did the doctor say? Yes, of course I'll set it up. I'll take care of everything for you!" she said sounding like her mind was going mile a minute. As I explained everything to her she began praying. Praying over the phone like the prayer warrior she was. I learned how to pray from Heather. She had prayed over me a number of times throughout my journey for recovery and this time was no different.

"I'll set everything up for you and call you Monday or Tuesday with a date. It will be this month."

"Ok. Thanks for everything Heather. From the bottom of my heart, thank you so much."

"You're a warrior Christina. You are a mighty child of the great I Am. He will not forsake you. Trust me on this. I feel it."

"I love your face."

"I love yours too" she said as we hung up.

It was Saturday night April 15th, 2017 and the night air was still. A calming swept over me and again, I felt serenity. Everything was falling into place and I thanked God once again before I went to sleep for everything he had given me and everything he had taken away. But, He wasn't done with me yet. He was still going to prove to me that there is no power greater than the presence of the great Lion of Judah.

***

Heather called me that next Tuesday night and told me I was to be baptized by the Worship Pastor that I had requested that next Sunday which would be April 23rd ·2017. It was a solemn feeling and an elated feeling all at the same time. You see, when you get baptized its literally a public display and confession of your sins to God and in turn they get washed away and you are reborn as they say into Gods Family. I had no idea how I would feel afterwards. All I knew at the time was that it was something that I had to do before I couldn't. The week leading up to my baptism was very trying at the beginning. Then as I said that God wasn't done with me yet, he once again bathed me in His son's blood and the grace and mercy of the Lord washed over me yet again. It was Thursday morning on my way to work and the phone rang.

"Christina Giordano please?" the voice on the other end said rather formally as I picked up the phone.

"This is her. How can I help you?" I said politely which was a far cry from the way I used to answer the phone.

"This is Dr. Ramirez's' office. Please hold the line as he would like to speak to you." She said putting me on hold without giving me a chance to respond.

"Hi Christina, Dr. Ramirez here. I'd like to talk to you about something."

"Oh God what now?"

"It's all good, don't get stressed that's not good for your liver. I want to try a different pharmacy to try and get you approved for the treatment."

"Oh God Doc. I don't know. I've been denied three times. I'm actually making funeral arrangements with my sister! Honestly, I don't think I want to go through having to get my hopes up and let down by another rejection. That's not good for my liver either."

"Please, Christina. I found a pharmacy up in Tampa that because of your low viral load they say you only need eight weeks of treatment instead of twelve. They are very confident they can get it for you." After he badgered me for about ten to fifteen minutes explaining why I needed to set myself up for another rejection, I gave in.

"Oh geez! Ok! Ok! Go for it. But I'm not getting my hopes up. I have my urn picked out already for crying out loud!"

"Honestly, Miss Giordano, I really hope you didn't put a deposit on it because I don't think you are going to need it."

"You're funny Doc."

With that we hung up and as I sat at the stop light down the street from work, I thought to myself, "Here we go again Christina. Strap yourself in because you're headed for another go around." I also prayed again, but this time my prayers were different. It was an overcast day and I remember sitting in my car and asking God for his favor and mercy. "Lord, if this is the time let it be now. Let your will over my life prevail. Please do not forsake me this time." As I said those words, the sun came out and the phone rang again.

"Christina Giordano, please?"

"This is her."

"Hi, this is Deborah I am the head pharmacist at Med Script Pharmacy in Tampa. I have to ask you a few questions do you have time?"

"Wow! That was fast! I just hung up the phone with my doctor."

"Yes, I told Dr. Ramirez that I would call you right away as he explained your hesitancy with going a fourth round trying to get treatment. I want to tell you that I'm in your corner. Your viral load is so low and you got it down so fast that I think the way I present everything to the pharmaceutical company and insurance you will get treatment and close to very little to no out of pocket expense."

"Oh Lord have mercy! That's an expensive treatment! How are you going to do that?"

"You let me worry about that. Given your financial status you qualify for assistance as well."

So, we went through the whole questionnaire that consisted of financial, medical, dietary supplements I was taking and personal information. At the end of our conversation, I felt slightly hopeful although deep down inside, I had no hope at all except the hope in God that He was going to do what He saw fit for me.

"Ok Christina, I have all the information I need. You should be hearing back from me within a day or two. In the meantime, drink at least fifty-four ounces of water and keep that liver clean."

"Yes ma'am!"

No sooner did we hang up, what seemed to be about two minutes later the phone rang again. It was the busiest morning for personal phone calls I had ever encountered.

"Hello?" I said with a big sigh. At this point all these phone calls had followed me into work and even though the new job yielded the best bosses who were totally understanding of my medical needs and gave me 100% of their support, it felt awkward that they actually let me take the phone calls because no one I had ever worked for had ever showed me that much respect.

"Christina, it's Deborah from Medi Scripts," she said as I held my breath. "Honey, you've been approved and you qualified for 100% financial assistance!"

"Oh my God! Oh my God! Praise the Lord! My God's not dead He is surely alive! Lord have mercy on my soul! Oh Lord how can it be?" I fell to my knees in my office.

"Oh, Christina I am so Happy for you! Hold on just one minute. I want to see if we have the Harvoni in stock. If we do I can have it in your hands tomorrow at 9am. If not, you'll have to wait until Monday."

"Oh my God, thank you so much! Yes, I'll hold."

A wave of light came over me as I was kneeling on the floor of my office. A light and a warmth that I had felt before. When I was laying in that hospital bed asking my God and my Savior for redemption of all my sins. This time the light lit my heart up and that light has remained ever since that day.

"Christina, I have it in stock. You'll have the treatment in your hands at nine o'clock tomorrow morning."

"Oh, thank you so much Deborah. You are an angel sent from God. Thank you so much for believing in me."

***

We went through the whole instruction on how to take the treatment. It would be one pill every day for eight weeks and as I added it up in my head, it would be a grand total of $73,000.00 that I was being granted. That was crazy and overwhelming but I was so thankful. To this day I can never thank Dr. Ramirez enough for never giving up even when I had and to Deborah for believing that I was a good enough person to receive a second chance at life. I wasn't going to let anyone down, not even myself. Friday morning came and as promised, Federal Express showed up at work at nine o'clock on the dot and at 9:17 a.m. I took my first pill of Harvoni. I didn't tell anyone about getting approved which I kind of felt bad about because all everyone knew was that I was getting baptized Sunday and in about year

I wasn't going to be here anymore. I wanted to wait and announce it at my baptism. I did post on Facebook a simple post though, it read, "Day 1 9:17am". Some people liked it, but nobody knew what it meant. Then my sister called.

"Hey, sissy!" I said in a happy voice.

"Hey," she said sternly, "I saw your post. What does that mean? Are you ok?"

"Yes! I'm great! How about you?"

"Christina, what does that mean?" she was getting agitated and I started laughing as she got more agitated from me giggling.

"Today at 9:17 a.m., I took my first pill of Harvoni. I got approved for treatment!"

"Get the fuck out! Praise Jesus!"

"D.D.! I hardly think using an F-bomb and the name Jesus in the same sentence is suitable!" I said laughing even harder. My sister can get confused sometimes. Then she just went on praising our Lord and thanking Him for all kind of things.

We hung up with the regular I love you and I went about my day at work after setting my phone alarm for 9:17 am every day for the next eight weeks.

***

On the way home from work as I was praying and thanking God for everything in my life which included giving me life, I started to think about my baptism that was coming up. God made everything perfect in His perfect timing and I was to finally be baptized knowing that the grace and mercy of God had delivered me from my sins. What a great full circle it had been. I started to think about the day my mother died, the day I ran into the Catholic church down the street and renounced my faith in Him. The almighty one who just eight hours ago delivered me from my death sentence and gave me life again. Then as sure as my heart was beating, a rush of the brightest light came over me, I can't begin to explain it. It wasn't like the sun coming out or the hand of God on my heart. It was like the Holy Spirit filled my entire body with a light so bright. I started to get goose bumps and the hair on my arms stood straight up. I had just realized what Sunday was going to be. Sundays date was April 23rd, 2017.

"Oh my God!" I screamed, "I have to call someone and tell them! Who do I call?" I was screaming to myself in my car. People were looking at me at the stop light like I was a crazy woman!

"Lisa! I have to call Lisa!"

As I calmly called not just my editor of this book but my confidant, my friend and my sister in Christ, my anxiety skyrocketed. The still beaming light I felt through my body was covering me from head to toe. As she answered the phone I cut her off from her hello.

"Lisa, I have to tell you something and don't say a word until I'm done."

"Ok dude, you alright?" She is so California.

"Yeah! I'm fine! Just hear me out. Remember in the chapter where I'm explaining how I ran into the Catholic church and renounced my faith when my mom died?"

"Yeah?"

"Remember what the date was that I did that?"

"No, I would have to re-read it."

"Lisa, it was April 23rd, 1992. Lisa, I'm getting baptized April 23rd, 2017. Lisa, twenty-five years to the day later. I didn't realize it until now! It didn't dawn on me when Heather gave me the date!"

"Oh my God, dude!" She's so California, "That's Gods work right there and no one else's! Praise Jesus! Dude, I got goose bumps on my whole body right now! This doesn't happen to people Christina!"

"I know!" We were both teary eyed at this point and then I had to tell her. "Lisa, there's more though."

"Lord I don't know if I can take much more than that!"

"Lisa, I got the cure. I took the first pill this morning at 9:17."

"What!" Her scream deafened me but I love how she gets excited about stuff.

"And it didn't cost me anything. I got all the financial aid and my insurance paid the rest."

"Oh my God! Dude!" Lord have mercy she is so California! "You are so bathed in the blood of Jesus Christ right now you have no idea! Oh, praise Jesus! You have been washed and bathed with God's grace, I can't even stand it it's so awesome! Christina, this doesn't happen to people, unless there's a 100% faith in Him! In the past six months, I have witnessed so many miracles in you. It's ridiculous dude! This just doesn't happen every day. You are favored, chosen and a witness to His glory. Dude, you have got to put this in the book, and I'm going to help you as much as I can, if you'll let me!"

We both laughed and cried and the joy and praise coming out of us would make angels sing. It was one of my fondest memories of this journey. It was one of those days you just could never forget. And low and behold, I put it in the book and have grown very fond of the word "Dude".

***

Sunday came and I decided to wear my favorite dress to get baptized in. As usual I attended the eleven o'clock service and right after that, noon to be exact, I would be washing away all my sins in the big fountain just outside of the worship center. I invited some friends but only two showed up; Cheryl and Denise who are two of my best friends in the world. Denise as usual had her camera in hand and Cheryl with her phone taking video as they both knew there was some kind of announcement but had no idea what it was. Pastor Adam talked me through everything as I made proclamation of the confessions of my sins. Then as I was laid back into the water, I heard the voice of God, "It is finished". It was the words He spoke before He took His last breath on the cross. But when I heard those words under the water it was like a heavy weight left my body and I felt as light as a feather. Pastor Adam and his assistant Richard pulled me out of the water and as every drop left my body so did it feel like every sin was left in that fountain. As I opened my eyes on that over cast morning, again, the heavens opened up and the sun was shining as bright as could be. God did favor me. He forgave me and bestowed victory on me. I was no longer a victim of fate. My will and my life I had completely turned over to the will of God.

As Cheryl kept the video going, I humbly told the on lookers of what my fate had been and what it had now become. I claimed my victory over Satan as I told Denise and Cheryl while standing in the fountain that I had been granted the treatment cure for my affliction and that I had been also granted a second chance at life. Everyone rejoiced and Cheryl and Denise yelled their Halleluiahs with tears in their eyes as now they knew their friend was no longer going to carry the death sentence that she was handed 5 months prior. I was going to live. I was going to live my life the way God intended it to be.

***

The meaning of the words, *Gods Not Dead,* does not imply that he ever was. Some Christians do not like that saying as it implies that new believers at one point thought he was. The saying comes from a movie and a song by the Christian Rock band, *The Newsboys,* both consequently called *God's Not Dead.* It is the implication of a God that is always working for your good. Sometimes you may not see and because of this, some feel that God has abandoned them, thus God died in them. He lays trials and tribulations on you to increase your faith. To bring you closer to Him. By doing this he is also concocting a miracle for you to witness. In my case, it was a series of miracles. My point is, I have several people that talk to me and somehow find their strength by doing that. I wouldn't call myself a martyr because I stopped crying the blues a while ago when things go bad. I try to carry Gods word to people who will listen. The miracles he has performed in my life are immense. I still to this day always thank him for everything he has given me and everything he has taken away. He keeps taking care of me when I don't deserve it. I think that's one of the biggest issues with people that I see. If they can't see it or touch it, it simply does not exist to them. The Bible teaches us to walk by faith and not by sight. Once you submit and learn how to do that, there's some incredible things that you will be witness to. One of those amazing things is actually seeing the will of God work in the most peculiar ways. I witness people all the time thinking the world owes them something. Heck, I used to be one of them. But the truth is, sobriety and faith are not things that are handed to you. They both require work. God wants nothing more in return for His good favor except a relationship with you. While you sit there and curse your enemies, He forgives them. Honestly, if God forgives them, who are you not to? If you just be still and listen to His voice, you will never have to worry about anything. There are six elements to a peaceful life. They are joy, gentleness, prayer, gratitude, your thoughts and your mentors.

Joy is a choice you make and God is bigger than your circumstance. Gentleness is rare and it will bring peace to all that you do. Prayer is the opposite of worry. There's nothing in the world that God can't do. Gratitude is thanksgiving which is a prayerful request for gratitude. You cannot find peace if you don't have gratitude. Your thoughts are the choices you make. If you focus on the positive and speak the truth, your thoughts become a discipline. Your mentors are who you are going to learn from. They are who you allow into your life. The old saying goes, "You are the company you keep". Therefore, choose your mentors wisely.

***

I found that following these six steps will lead to a peaceful life. Don't let someone decide that you deserve a death sentence. Don't let people scare you into submission. The Armor of God will always adorn you. Whom shall you fear? No one except God, and I don't mean that literally. Fearing God is trusting Him, having Faith in Him that no matter what is going on, doubt has no room in you. Peace is the result of your choices. It's up to you if you will allow the God of Peace to be with you. I kept praying for all the ones that had transgressed against me. It brought me peace. Even though I knew I would never see any of them ever again, or so I thought.

CHAPTER 13

ENJOY THE JOURNEY

***

But those who hope in the Lord shall renew their strength. They will soar on wings like eagles; they will run and not grow weary, they will walk and not grow faint.
~ *Isaiah 40:31*

When you get baptized, even though it's an amazing feeling to leave your sins in a big pool of water, the reality is you have to be prepared for the aftermath. Satan gets upset when you find your faith and hope in God and His "Word of Life", but he gets down right angry when you get baptized. Although you think you are prepared, you have no idea what you're in for. You have to be on your guard because that's the moment Satan starts working over-time. The very things you thought you put to rest will come back to tempt you in ways you didn't think would ever happen again. People that you deleted from your life will often show up proclaiming their innocence. The ones that crucified you will all of a sudden believe in you. Although some of these incidences are genuine, you must discern truth from the lies and deceit. A wolf will sometimes cloak themselves in sheep's clothing to gain your favor for their own warped desires. It is in that instance, when you're scared or unsure that you ask for Gods will to take over. If your relationship with Him is what it should be, that's when He tests your faith and mercy on another who may need it.

***

During my eight weeks of treatment, life seemed to take on a whole new meaning. I was clean and sober, I was happy and leading the life I always wanted. I started thinking like a victor and not a victim. Once I changed my thought process everything started to fall perfectly in place. However, getting financially on track seemed to be a problem. It would take me over a year to get financially secure to the point where I wasn't worrying about how I was going to pay my rent and wasn't worrying where my next meal was coming from. With perseverance and a lot of going to bed hungry, it makes me appreciate where I am today; financially, emotionally, physically, mentally and spiritually fit. I would go to my weekly NA meetings on Thursday nights and attend church every Sunday morning faithfully, every time asking and praying to God not to forsake me. When I look back now, those hard times were shaping me into becoming the person I truly am. While I continued to pray for myself, I also continued to pray for Andy and Matt. From what I'd heard through the grapevine of trusted sources, they were still active in their addictions of drugs and alcohol. I prayed so hard for God to have mercy on them. I once loved Matt and although he chose other women and drugs over me, that still didn't shut down the fact that I once loved him and still to this day care about him. Andy on the other hand was a different story. He kept using and abusing his charm to get what he wanted which was manipulating people, stealing from them and continuing to shoot his drugs up. I felt pity for him. He once was a very kind and talented man and now, he had wasted away into a dark abyss. He fell down that rabbit hole and while chastising me for coming out of it, he was headed down a darker path. I've learned to worry about my own 'inventory' and not dote on someone else's misfortunes. You can never help someone who doesn't want to be helped and you have to at some point remove yourself from people who are always depressed and doing absolutely nothing about it except wallow in their depression especially if you are an addict. When we first enter into sobriety and all is going exceedingly glorious, we sometimes over compensate our addiction and try to save the world. I realized I couldn't do this as it would affect my recovery. I would try to comfort certain friends that would come to me for prayer but in the end, they weren't praying for themselves. A program and faith only works if you work it. Recovery is constant. It is not presented to you on a silver platter. It didn't take you one day to mess yourself up, and it sure as heck isn't going to take you one day to straighten it all out. However, in time, perseverance, faith and dedication will pay off in the end. Trust me…I'm an addict.

***

Andy and I had a mutual friend in common, well a mutual 'party buddy' is a better word for it. Mark was a decent guy, heck I used to sell him drugs but that's beside the point. Mark was handsome as well and regarded as one of the best guitar players in our area. I had suspected he had gone down that same rabbit hole as I hadn't heard from him since before I got clean. Last time I'd seen him, he had a needle in his arm in my kitchen. One day out of the blue he called me and asked if we could go for coffee. I was surprised to hear from him as I knew that he was probably still friends with Andy. After all, it's all about people, places and things and he was a people. Nevertheless, I acquiesce to meet him and surprisingly things went quite well. He told me what had happened to him and the reason for him contacting me was to make an amends with me which in my eyes, was purely financial as he never deliberately hurt me in any way. He had got drugs from me on more than one occasion and never paid me. It was a total of $180.00. But that was drug money now.; dirty money if you will and frankly, I didn't want that back. I suggested he make a $180.00 donation to a charity of his choice to release that financial amends from himself because I had already forgiven him for it. Again, not for him to receive forgiveness from me, but for myself to continue on my path of serenity. He had over dosed and went to rehab and was now clean and going to meetings and living in a half-way house trying to better himself and his life. We spoke about a lot of things that day including the Bible. I'd never known he was a walking scripture hub. This man had scripture memorized for everything we said and talked about. We also talked about Andy. Mark was in the same half-way house as where Andy had been only Andy wasn't there anymore. He had been kicked out for coming back to the house high and well, you just don't do that at a half-way house. I felt bad for Andy but mostly I for a moment got mad at God. Here I was spending my prayers on Andy when God wasn't doing anything for him. Then as I always do, I become still and listen to His voice. "Christina, you can't help someone that doesn't want to help themselves", That is such an old worn out saying but it's so true. Mark went on to say that he was in a better place now with God and himself and I thought, this is perfect! He loves God, he's sober and we have our sobriety in common and he is someone I could spend my time with. Mark and I hung out together every chance we got. On Saturdays, we would have dinner at my house and watch a movie and then I would drive him back to the half-way house. On Sunday, I would pick him up and we would go to church together and then after we would have lunch on occasion. We did this for a several months. We spoke about possibly having a relationship a few times but his recovery was important to me and him being very new in the recovery program, I had told him that we should wait until he had some clean-time and then revisit the possibility again in six months. During this time I started to experience life outside the four walls of my apartment. The world still scared me but I was making a conscious effort to eradicate that feeling.

***

Then, one Sunday after church we had lunch and he invited me to his CA meeting. CA stands for Cocaine Anonymous. It's more spiritually driven like Alcoholics Anonymous is and I had never gone to one so it would be a nice change in scenery and people. When I dropped him off at his house, we were saying our good-byes when suddenly out of the corner of my eye I saw a person moving. It was Andy. I hadn't seen him in almost a year. He was so skinny, gaunt and sickly looking, so much so it broke my heart to see him like that. Mark had told me that Andy had overdosed and had returned to the half-way house to try sobriety again. As Mark saw me look away with disgust he said, "Christina, you and Andy are going to have to eventually put the bad blood between you to rest. You both are friends of mine and I won't choose."

"Mark, I would never expect you to. Besides, I don't hold any ill will against Andy. I own my part in all that drama. I know the choices I made were my choices. It just makes me sad and sick at the same time to see that is was what I used to look like and this is what has become of him."

"Yes," Mark said, "But his choice to shoot you up and deliberately give you the Hepatitis C was *his* bad choice and judgement and that is something he will live with and eventually will have to make amends to if he wants to stay clean."

"Mark, Andy has no remorse. He could care less what he gives anybody. Andy has always been about Andy no matter what death sentence he dishes out to people. The difference is that I forgive him where as someone else might not have."

"Well, the tension needs to be lifted."

"Mark, he's been clean and sober only a few weeks if that. I doubt he's gotten through step one, let alone skipping to step nine!" I said referencing the *12 Steps of Sobriety*.

"No, he hasn't been sober that long, true. But God will figure it out and when He does I'm sure you'll be the first to know. I'm going to pray on it."

"You do that buddy." I said with a chuckle, "I'll see you at the CA meeting at five."

"Ok," he said getting out of my car. "Hey, can you pick me up? I got a ride home but I need a ride there."

"Sure!" I said hesitating at first. This taxi service stuff was becoming a real pain in the rear end.

With a sigh and a final glance at Andy sitting under a tree in the yard smoking a cigarette, I put the car in reverse. As I looked up to turn around to back up, Andy and I locked eyes. My hair stood on end and my heart started palpitating. Not because of feelings or anything it was a flashback. The veins in my arms started to ache and itch. Oh man, I didn't like this feeling at all. My arms felt like little needles were pricking my skin. It was a horrible sensation. I had to get out of that driveway and I couldn't back up fast enough. It was all the memories of the time I spent with Andy that flooded my mind all at once. All I could do was scream in the car on the way home. Be gone satan! My life has no room for you here. Not in my head, not in my home, not in any fiber of my being. I rebuke you in the name of my Lord and Savior Jesus Christ!" I repeated this over and over again until I got to my house and ran inside slamming the door behind be like someone was after me. Someone was after me alright. It was Satan. Satan brought the worst thing he knew possible to get to me. As I locked the door behind me I ran into my prayer room and began to engage in spiritual warfare. When I rage out and go to war now, I enter the war room as a warrior of Christ. Not a warrior against Christ. As much as I praise God for everything there needs to be a balance. You see, everything isn't all sunshine and lollipops. For so long even after I got sober and cured from Hepatitis C, I was looking through rose-colored glasses. You need to keep a balance of Praise for the Lord and spiritual warfare against evil otherwise there's no point in doing any of it. Spiritual warfare keeps us alert and mindful of the enemy who is always at work devising his next plan of attack. Praise and prayer keep us mindful that God is always at work for our protection and for our good. As I entered the prayer room, I began screaming out about how much I detest the devil, but I also praised God for His glory and named myself the victor over the evil that had literally almost swallowed me up while sitting in that drive way. If I was going to be friends and hang out with Mark, I would have to come to the realization that as long as Andy lived in the same halfway-house I would have to get my head together. I was dreading having to go back there and pick Mark up for the meeting later on but after this I knew I had to face those demons. I knew I was strong enough to do it. I had that Armor of God wrapped around me tight and the evil that protruded from that house like a bad infection of the earth was not ever going to bring me down again. I was a warrior, it was time to start acting like one.

***

I picked Mark up at five o'clock as promised. Did I mention the taxi service thing was getting old? I told Mark what I'd gone through earlier that afternoon after I left him, and then he told me how angry Andy was.

"Boy Andy was pissed after you left today."

"I can imagine. What did he say?"

"Ha! You mean what did he *not* say? He was screaming, yelling and throwing a fit saying stuff like, 'How could you hang around that bitch.', and 'Why did you have to pick her?' Heck, at one point he raised his fist wanting to hit me!"

"Mark, he does know that you're like an eight degree or whatever black belt and you could kill him, right? I mean jeez, he's so skinny and sickly looking right now you could probably flick him in the forehead and knock him out."

"Christina, I'm an eight- degree whatever black belt. I can flick anyone in the forehead and knock them out." He said sarcastically.

"Asshole." I retorted back with a smirk. He was such a smart ass sometimes but as the days went by that we hung out together, he got better looking and always made me laugh and smile.

"Seriously though, I grabbed him and told him, 'Andy, calm the fuck down. She is fucking praying for you man! What person do you know that was dealt a death sentence that keeps the person that almost killed them in their prayers? Who? No one! She's been praying for you since she found out you infected her with Hepatitis C! And you never once asked how she was doing! NO! You are a fucking selfish asshole. You crucified her! She did a lot for you. She put clothes on your back when you didn't have any! She fed you when you were hungry! She gave you a place to sleep when you were homeless! And all you did was lie, cheat and steal from her! Then to top it all off, you knowingly gave her a deadly disease and she still prays for you? What the fuck is your problem with her, better with *you*?' Oh yeah, I laced into him alright!" Mark said.

"Holy cow! You said all that to him?"

"Damn right I did. Listen Christina, I may be an egotistical asshole but I care about you and what Andy did to you is wrong. Point blank. But the difference is in all this is that you admit your fault in it whereas Andy hasn't, at least not yet."

"You mean won't, nor ever will. But that's not my journey. That's his"

"Oh no, I think he figured it out after I got done letting him have it."

"How do you mean?" I asked curiously.

"Well, after I got done lacing into him he looked me straight in the eyes and went down to his knees and started crying like a baby."

"Oh my God!"

"Yeah. Then he looked up at me and said, 'Mark, I almost killed her. Oh my God I almost killed her'. Christina, I think he finally gets it. He almost took someone's life and while Andy is all about Andy, I mean, come on, we are all about ourselves. We're addicts. It's one of our characteristic flaws. I think he realized at that point the damage he caused and the catastrophe that could've happened. Honestly Christina, I'm impressed with your character as a human being. I told him, 'Man she forgives you. You're lucky you didn't get charged with attempted murder. That woman forgave you!'

With Marks words, I was dumb founded. Nobody had stuck up for me like that through this whole ordeal. Mark wasn't even there when it all went down almost a year prior. He never saw any of it. But he knew. He knew Andy like the back of his hand and what he's capable of. He knew I was not the person I was before all of this went down. Nor was I now the person I was after all I've been through. I was different.

"Christina, you and your sobriety and where you are in life is way up here," as he raised his hand over his head, "Me and Andy aren't there yet and for you and I to have a relationship, I've got to play catch up." Lord have mercy, where was this conversation going now?

"Dude," I was so going to put a stop to the direction of this, "I totally get that. I have more clean time than you. Let's not worry about that. As our motto says, *'One Day at a Time'*, okay?"

"Okay." He responded in a relieved tone.

"Okay then. Let's go play with our fellow drug addicts." I said sarcastically

"Girl, that isn't right." We both started laughing.

That night as I was falling asleep, I was filled up with a huge amount of calmness inside my heart. It felt like more serenity was coming into my life. What started out as a war earlier in the day, ended with a serene outcome. Spiritual war fare serves two purposes. The first to ward off evil. To put an end to the chaotic mess that gets Satan's rock off, so to speak. The second is, it is a catalyst to make way for Gods will to be done. This day was the perfect example of that. It was another victory notch in the belt of truth which is part of the Armor of God. God truly answered my prayers. I knew this journey wasn't over yet. Even though my path was straight, my life was coming together and my mind was clear. However, I felt like something was left unfinished. Mark was right. I needed closure. Though I had forgiven Andy and had moved on, it wasn't enough. As I thought back to the beginning of this crazy journey into my second chance at life, again the thought came up that it wasn't enough. But this time, it wasn't me that wasn't enough. It was more of what I was doing was not enough. I had more to do. God had put more in my path to complete. However, the worst thing you could ever do is rush God's will for an outcome. So, I just sat back and relaxed. I prayed for patience and perseverance at the same time. Then suddenly, like watching the plot line of your favorite movie unfold so did Gods will. It was all again, in His perfect timing.

***

It was a beautiful hot sunny day at the end of July 2017 in Southwest Florida. I was 11 months clean, cured of Hepatitis C and feeling the strongest and healthiest I have ever felt. The sky was clear and Mark was finally at a place in his life where he was moving out of the halfway-house and into a condo in Cape Coral. I was so happy for him because he worked really hard at his sobriety and recovery and had prevailed. It was moving day and as usual, my taxi cab was running that day so I told him I would help him move his stuff out of the house and to his new place which just happened to be conveniently down the street from me. He was all excited as well and so after he was off work, I met him at the halfway-house and waited for him to start bringing his things out. There wasn't much because he had been homeless before this and pretty much just had his clothes, his bible, his guitar and his bike to load up. But he had to get it all out himself as I was not allowed inside due to the fact that no one was allowed inside the house if you didn't live there. As I sat in my car waiting for him, I was rocking out to my favorite Christian Rock station, singing away when I looked up and there he was; Andy. He came out the back door carrying a laundry basket full of clothes, heading to the laundry room in the backyard. He saw me sitting in my car but continued walking on by. As I watched him put his clothes into the washing machine and start it, I remembered a time when he had folded laundry at my house and had everything nicely piled on the dining room table. I teased him that day about doing that good deed only because he wanted to get into my panties. I chuckled to myself at the memory of a rare moment in time that we both smiled without being high. Those days were long gone now. I would no longer be the woman that he remembered. In fact, I was no longer the woman anybody would remember.

The tension was in the air that day. I had my sunglasses on so he couldn't really see if I was looking at him or not, but he was surely looking at me. I pretended to look down at my phone while keeping an eye on him the whole time. As Mark emerged from the house several times packing my car to the hilt of this and that, he stopped to talk to Andy for a few times. I have no idea about what but it seemed a bit intense. Finally, as Mark brought out the last bit of his belongings, we arranged everything perfectly so it all fit. It was now time to go.

"Hold on Christina, I want to say good-bye to everyone."

"Ok, I'll wait here." I said standing outside my driver side door.

Mark went up to everyone sitting outside and shook their hands, knuckle bumped and did the man hug thing. Then, as he came to Andy their hands stretched out to each other and they embraced. It was heart felt as Mark was a mentor for Andy to look up to because of their friendship and while Mark was moving onto the next stage of his life, Andy was just at the beginning coming off of an almost deadly relapse. I watched the two men hug and lowered my head solemnly. When I looked back up Mark had made his way back to the passenger door about to get in the car when I glanced at Andy staring at me. I saw a look on Andy's face that I thought I would never see; remorse. My lips parted slightly as I caught my breath and looked back at him. I only had to hear the one word that came out of his mouth. It was almost a whisper.

"Christina."

I looked down at the ground so confused not knowing what to do next. So many thoughts went through my head and at warp speed, I didn't have enough time to contemplate on any of them. I stomped the ground with my foot and started to cry as I took off half running in Andy's direction. As I got closer he started running in my direction, meeting on middle ground. He scooped me up into his arms and held me for what seemed like a lifetime. Cradling the back of my head in his hand and the other wrapped around me tight. His face buried into my neck as we both took in a deep breath let out by a big sigh. It was a sigh of relief for both of us. We were both crying and couldn't let each other go.

"You look good Andy." Was the only thing I could think of saying as he'd gained a little bit of weight and started to look healthy again.

"Thanks, you do too. In fact, you look amazing." He said through his tears.

"Oh Andy. Take care of yourself. I prayed so hard for you to get clean and to find your peace."

"I am Christina. I'm finally finding my peace and staying clean for myself. Christina, I'm so sorry I hurt you. Please forgive me." Andy spoke with tears and conviction in his voice that I had never heard from him before. As I backed away from him to look at his face. I put both my hands up to him holding his still handsome face and looking him straight into his blue eyes.

"Andy, I forgave you from what seems like such a long time ago," I said as a smile ran across my tear stained face, "It's now time for you to forgive yourself."

With my words Andy lowered his head and began to cry. I'd never seen him humbled in the face of forgiveness. I lifted his face to mine and threw my arms around him one last time.

"Someday we will have to sit down and talk. But not now. You aren't ready. I don't think either of us are."

"When we're both ready." He replied.

I giggled, "Yeah, when we're both ready."

With that we said our goodbyes to each other. Mark and I got in my car and headed on our way. As we made our approach to the Fort Myers Bridge, Mark finally broke the silence.

"You're awfully quiet," he said.

"I suppose I'm just taking it all in. Kind of basking in the serenity of what just happened, you know?" I said in a thoughtful tone. "You were right Mark. I needed that closure and I think Andy did too."

"Yes, you did. You both did." There was a short pause. "So, how do you feel?"

I smiled and looked at Mark. Damn he was handsome today.

"Does it seem overly bright out here today or is it just my imagination?" I asked him.

"Girl! You know just as well as I do. That's Gods glory shining down on us today!"

We both looked at each other with big smiles on our face and as we traveled over the Fort Myers Bridge on that overly beautiful and brilliant sunny day in July 2017. That was a day I will surely never forget. Just as Mark turned the radio up on that favorite Christian Rock station, the song 'God's Not Dead', by *The Newsboys* came on. We sang the chorus at the top of our lungs for the whole world to hear. "God's Not Dead He's surely alive! He's living on the inside roaring like a lion.", as we sang with joy and praise! It was the most perfect day, God's pure light shined extra bright on three people's lives that day. Mark, Andy and I were no longer living in bleakness of a dreaded long dark rabbit hole that once consumed us. And as for me, I was finally free.

***

When you make the choice to clean yourself up it's not just you that gets cleaned up. Everything around you is magnificent, a sort of conglomerate of miracles. When you forgive yourself, you find that no matter what trials and tribulations try to knock you down, keeping a positive attitude not only heals your life, but it has a profound effect on your health and the world around you. I can look in the mirror now and be proud of the woman I am today. I've learned to look at myself in a positive light. I am beautiful, fierce, worthy, I am enough and most importantly, I am a child of God. I don't have to hide behind a mask or stand on stage so I can pretend to be someone that I am not. I'm me now. I'm the person I was created to be. I don't have many friends anymore but I've learned it's about quality, not quantity and those who were your friends when times were flying high were only there to bask in your limelight. God made your light for you and only you. Bask in your own limelight! Life is truly what you make of it. If you are lucky enough to get that second chance at life, to really know what your purpose is then take it and run with it. You only get this one life to do it. Then when you are still and you hear the voice of God on your heart, listen to Him. Once you turn your 'can not's' into 'can do's' you'll see infinite glory and grace at work within you. He is constantly making everything new and working for your benefit. It doesn't matter where you come from, what conditions you grew up in or even where you are now. He's always there you just have to stop, be still and turn around. Faith is the step you take to get through the door of hope to get to God's love that is on the other side. When you defy the odds, God will turn your scars into stars. His endless pursuit of you will never cease. Then, when you do stop and turn around, you can see Him, you can feel Him and you can hear Him. And these things are my dear friends, *The Ultimate High*.

The End

Because Jesus was raised from the dead, we've been given a brand-new life and have everything to live for, including a future in heaven – and the future starts now!
~ 1 Peter 1:3

EPILOGUE

You have been set apart and chosen for His purpose ~Deuteronomy 14:2

It has been almost year since that bright brilliant day in July 2017. I never saw Andy again after that day. My one year celebration of sobriety came and went and my relationship with God got even stronger. Mark and I carried on for about two months more and then he just faded out of my life to start dating someone else. I like to think now, he didn't think he was enough for me. At first the thoughts of not being enough came into my head but quickly dissipated as there is not one person on this earth that can dictate how you are going to feel. Your feelings are your own and it's up to you and you alone to decide how you will deal with them. While I keep to my celibacy and sobriety, I also keep to myself.

Kimberly Bigelow, my third angel of The Magnificent Seven had a beautiful baby boy. Cindy went on tour with a National band. Cheryl and I see each other every week for lunch, dinner or a Christian rock concert. And a lot of people that crucified me came back around to apologize. I accepted their apologies and moved on. Some of them had been infected with Hepatitis C because of the same obvious reason I had been and realized I was telling the truth because now it had happened to them. Some were manipulated like I was and thought they were immortal as well. I prayed for them. I didn't go out of my way for them, but I prayed for them. Everything can be forgiven but not everything can be forgotten. Matt even got a hold of me after nineteen months to ask if I still had his CD's. Really? After 19 months he couldn't think of a better question to try and make contact with me? I never answered him. Besides, those CD's got thrown out in the garbage with the rest of the memories of the past that I didn't need taking up space in my apartment or my mind.

Today I'm in a beautiful place. I found my peace. Life won't always be sunshine and lollipops, in fact it rarely is but with the grace that has been gifted to me by God, I know anything is possible. I didn't do anything to deserve it and I sure as heck still make mistakes. The one amazing thing that really gets me though now is the fact that I can go to the grocery store and spend the same amount on food as I did on a gram of cocaine and that food feeds me for two weeks! That is just one of the very small things that totally amazes me. There are so many blessings in life and I witness them on a daily basis now. I watch people I once knew as hopeless addicts find God. Every time someone asks me if they could come to church with me it makes my heart happy. I've watched several people from the old days put the needle down to give their life to the Lord. They are far and few between but for the few that do, it fills my heart with joy.

They say now that I am a "Hope Dealer", I kind of like that. They call me an inspiration; I like that too. But, that is by the grace of God. God had a purpose for me. I fell for a reason. I am now living proof that grace wins every time. My hope was that whoever reads this journey, they could also find hope. I was chosen by God to send a message. He used me in the most magnificent way. Someone had to take the fall to show another the light. That fall made me strong and courageous; at the same time, gave me the knowledge to help another. That's what this was all for.

My little Chihuahuas Ginger and Simone have aged in the last year and a half. They are twelve and thirteen respectively and I suppose the turbulent lifestyle I once had has taken its toll on them. I was given the most beautiful little Chihuahua/Shih-Tzu puppy from my friend Jon who had named her Faith appropriately as he had all intensions of giving her to me when she was born. She has become my new drug of choice so to speak as I am utterly obsessed with her. When I needed a friend, she gave me her sweet little paw. I in turn have many more wrinkles in my face now as well, but those wrinkles tell a story. They tell a story of hope, truth and the courage to face Satan himself. The world is still a scary place and I refuse to put myself, my health or my heart on the line to get hurt. I have morals now. I watch what I say and I think twice before I say it. On this fateful journey, I learned how to not only live again, it taught me how to be a lady. It taught me kindness and most of all how to forgive. You can never get passed your past without forgiveness. It will always hold you back. The scars have healed and so has my heart. I know now that I am enough and I will always be enough. I work my NA program, I go to church, I eat healthy and above all else, I am kind and courageous. That makes for a beautiful life.

I still get lonely sometimes, but we all do. I'm not telling you anything you don't already know. The difference is now, I immerse myself in healthy decisions. Whether it's going to the gym, reading a book, watching a Harry Potter marathon or simply creating art in my Bible. Even more simply than all of that, sometimes I just sit in the prayer room and pray. I still pray constantly. I still pray for Andy, Matt, Mark, my friends, my family, my pets, myself and especially for the still suffering addict. No matter where they are or who they may be. I pray for the addicts that are still of this earth suffering and all the ones who have left this earth and have found their peace in death. Addiction is not a pretty place and while the world crucifies us, they also have no idea how bad we want to be free of the pain and misery that we bring upon ourselves and our families. When we feel pain in active addiction, the drugs alter our chemical balance into thinking we need to numb the pain instead of work through it. However, working through that pain now as a sober addict, it challenges me to conquer those demons.

Personally, as I used to relish in pissing people off, I now get my rocks off pissing satan off. The better I do, the more aggravated he gets and therein lies the challenge. I absolutely love feeling my feelings now. It reminds me that I am human. It reminds me that I don't have to numb the pain anymore because I can achieve greatness and righteousness being sober. My mind and soul are clear and I conquer every battle on a level that is so much greater than I ever knew when I was messed up. Lack of self-control isn't fun but, it makes for one heck of a great story. The strategy of keeping your self-control is very simple; take it captive. Embrace what God has made you to be. He has blessed your life abundantly, you only need to stop and listen. In using your weaknesses as your strength, you become this mighty warrior, a child of God and nothing, absolutely nothing can ever condemn you. He gives us Devine Power to demolish our strongholds. God will always show up when you are in the pits to extend His hand and bring you out. He doesn't care about your past. You have this infinite choice to be a flight animal or a fight animal. The weak will run away from the way, the truth and the light. The strong remain steadfast and fight like the warrior God created them to be. Be that warrior!

God will always welcome you home. He sees you running to Him in the distance just like the protocol son and His arms are opened wide. Run to that light! Run as fast as you can. He will give you the gift of grace and bestow mercy on you just like he did me. He clothed me with dignity and gave me a future. Without Him I would not have made it and this story would never have been told. Find your peace as He's still working on you. God's not done with me yet either. He's still molding me into this beautiful masterpiece and for right now, I'm just unfinished.

These things I have spoken to you, so that in me you may find peace. In the world you have tribulation, But take courage; I have overcome the world. ~John 16:33

ABOUT THE AUTHOR

Christina still lives in Cape Coral with her Chihuahuas Ginger and Simone, her Chihuahua/Shih-Tzu, Faith and her Russian Siberian cat, Natasha. She's a construction project manager by trade and works for a glass fabrication company. She still plays the flute and her violins but not professionally anymore. Her future endeavors include activism in the mediation to make the drug Harvoni more accessible to patients who can't afford it for the treatment and cure of Hepatitis C as well as advocating and guidance for those who don't know where to begin to receive that help.

In her spare time, she journals and creates art in her Bible, attends church every Sunday and Narcotics Anonymous meetings weekly. She will also be embarking on a tour speaking to groups, churches and recovery centers across the U.S. as well as radio stations in the state of Florida to spread her message of courage, hope and strength to those in need.

And she loves God with all her heart.

53994980R00127

Made in the USA
Columbia, SC
24 March 2019